THE SACRED PENITENTIARIA

AND ITS

RELATIONS TO FACULTIES OF ORDINARIES AND PRIESTS

DISSERTATION

SUBMITTED TO THE FACULTY OF THEOLOGY OF THE CATHOLIC UNIVERSITY OF AMERICA

IN PARTIAL FULFILMENT OF THE REQUIREMENTS FOR THE DEGREE

DOCTOR OF CANON LAW

By WILLIAM J. KUBELBECK, S. T. B., J. C. L.
Catholic University of America

1918

Nihil Obstat:
✠ THOMAS J. SHAHAN, S. T. D.,
Censor Deputatus.

Imprimatur:
✠ J. CARD. GIBBONS,
Archiepiscopus Baltimorensis.

THE ROSARY PRESS, SOMERSET, OHIO
1918

THE SACRED PENITENTIARIA

AND ITS

RELATION TO FACULTIES OF ORDINARIES AND PRIESTS

CONTENTS

INTRODUCTION

The Sacred Penitentiaria, one of the three tribunals of the Roman Curia, was instituted for the purpose of giving absolution from sins and censures, of granting various dispensations, commutations of vows, condonations and other favors pertaining to the internal forum.

Benedict XIV in his constitution "Pastor bonus" (13 Apr. 1744) says: "Among the tribunals of the Roman Curia the Roman Pontiffs . . . have at a very early date, called into existence the Office of the Sacred Penitentiaria for the cleansing of sinners. Where the faithful of the Christian world can, either in person or by anonymous letter, secretly and gratuitously, obtain healing medicine for their spiritual ailments." There is an intimate relation between the S. Penitentiaria and the Sacrament of Penance. Both tribunals continue the work of "the Good Shepherd Christ Jesus, sent by the Father to seek the sheep that was lost. When He had found it and placed it upon His shoulders, He returned to heaven, but He gave to the vicars of His work the government of His entire flock, which He bought with a great price, leaving His example and precepts, that His flock be kept within moderate bounds of discipline, that those, who through the abuse of liberty have wandered from the path of salvation, be recalled to the fruits of justice and mercy" ("Pastor bonus"). The Church like a kind mother is ever ready to forgive the sins and crimes of her children. She relaxes the rigor of her laws and condones the faults of the penitent in imitation of her divine Founder *"the son of man, who came to seek and to save that which was lost"* (Luke 19, 10).

The New Code has changed little in the competency of the S. Penitentiaria. It will grant faculties for the internal forum in the future as it has done in the past. Many powers however, which were formerly enjoyed by the Ordinaries and priests in virtue of delegation, are now conceded them by law and hence it becomes necessary to study the the S. Penitentiaria in its relations to faculties of Ordinaries and priests. The scope of this dissertation is: to give a brief history of the S. Penitentiaria, to enumerate the faculties it had in the past and those it now enjoys, to indicate the powers of the Ordinaries and priests, and lastly, to point out the proper method of applying for and granting dispensations.

CHAPTER I

Origin of the Sacred Penitentiaria

Many able writers like Goeller, Denifle and Lang in Germany; Chouet, Villien in France; Lea and Haskins in this country, have rendered valuable service to the study of the Sacred Penitentiaria, but there still remains considerable work to be accomplished. How old is the Sacred Penitentiaria and what was its first constitution? These are questions, which have not been answered. What has thus far been found regarding the history of the Sacred Tribunal, is fragmentary and incomplete. Like all institutions it developed gradually.. Its beginnings reached back to the dawn of the Church, its government and competency were organized according to the needs of the times. Thus Benedict XII relates: "I have read in a certain old book, that the office of the Penitentiaries was exercised in olden times by Cardinal Priests, but when the work of the Church increased, these Cardinals no longer found time to hear confessions and hence Penitentiaries were instituted in their places, who were honored like Cardinals and were, so to say, Prelates of the whole world."[1] There are reasons for believing that the S. Penitentiaria had its orgin about the year 253 at the time of St. Cyprian and Pope St. Cornelius.[2] The persecutions during that time caused some of the faithful to weaken and lapse into apostasy and other sins reserved to the Pope. The Pope, because of his many administrative duties found little time to hear confessions and appointed ministers to represent him in the tribunal of Penance. This belief has some foundation, since the famous historians of the early Church, Socrates and Sozomen write, that Bishops appointed competent priests in the dioceses to hear confessions and absolve penitents from grievous sins.[3] According to the "Liber Pontificalis," Pope St. Marcellus (d. 309), after the persecution of Diocletian, divided the territorial administration of the Churches into twenty-five districts (tituli), appointing a presbyter over each, to prepare the catechumens for Baptism and to direct the performance of public penance. Pope Simplicius

---

[1] University of Rome MS., 119. f. 19. v.

[2] M. Lega, Praelectiones in Textum Juris Can. vol. 5.

[3] Socrates, Hist. Eccl. v. 19; Sozomen, Hist. Eccl. VII. 16.

(468-483) designated a week for the Churches of St. Peter, St. Paul and St. Lawrence the martyr, during which priests should administer the sacraments of Penance and Baptism.[4]

Penitentiaries are certainly more ancient in the East than in the West. All Oriental Churches had Penitentiaries in the fifth century. That of Constantinople has left us documents, which constitute a valuable contribution to the history of this subject matter. The Western Church did not have this institution at so early a date. Not until the Fourth Lateran Council (1215) were Penitentiaries appointed for all Cathedral Churches. Some authors, as for instance, De Luca, think that the office of the Penitentiary dates from the primitive Church.[5] Lega refers it to the time of Pope Cornelius (264), who is said to have appointed Penitentiaries "*pro lapsis*".[6] Other authors endeavor to show that Cardinals have elected Penitentiaries in Rome since the time of Benedict II (d. 685), but the origin remains doubtful. Benedict II and the "Liber Diurnus" have nothing on the subject.[7]

The office of the Penitentiaries gained in importance at the time of Alexander III (1159-1181). He was in the estimation of Rome, Italy and the whole of Christendom, "the Light of the Clergy, the Ornament of the Church, the Father of his city and of the whole world" and now ranks next to Innocent III as legislator of the Church in the Middle Ages.[8] With him began the renaissance of Canon Law. His reputation as a canonist began, when he was professor in Bologna and grew with the public attention given to his Commentary on the Decretum Cratianum, known as "Summa Magistri Rolandi".[9]

A thorough study of Canon Law caused men of learning to realize the full extent of papal powers and therewith the Pope's supreme jurisdiction in matters of dispensations and absolutions. Pope Alexander clearly expounded and explained the God-given powers of the Roman Pontiff and minutely indicated the faculties, which the Holy See enjoys. As a natural consequence of this doctrine we meet with the subsequent restriction of the episcopal authority and the different laws regulating their powers. The canonist John of God who wrote about this time (1250), speaks

---

[4] Anastasius Bibliothecarius in Simplicio. P. P.

[5] Relatio curiae rom. forensis, XII. Venice 1759.

[6] Prel. de judicio eccl. 263, note.

[7] Plettenberg, Notitia congr. et tribunal. curiae rom. Hildesheim 1593; Liber Diurnus, Duchesne Paris 1891.

[8] Card. Hergenroether Kirch. II, p. 497. Wernz, tit. XII, no. 237.

[9] Ed. Thaner, Insbruck 1875.

in detail of the different categories of sins, and of the confessors, priests, bishops and cardinals, who were competent to absolve from them.

In the early Church bishops alone reserved cases and rarely do we find papal reservations.[10] Not every bishop reserved sin and centures to himself, but only a few here and there. Thus the Counc. of York (Eborancence) a. 1195 cap. 11, imposes on perjurers the obligation to apply to the bishop for absolution.[11] The Synodal Constitution of Paris decreed that atrocious crimes, as homicide, sacrilege, sins against nature, incest, seduction of virgins, violence to clerics be reserved to the bishop.[12]. St. Thomas enumerates only five cases reserved to bishops.[13]

Isolated cases reserved to the Pope are found in the Penitential Books. The Holy See for example reserved the power of dispensing from a pilgrimage to Rome in expiation for the crime of killing a cleric.[14] As early as the ninth century excommunication was inflicted on those who injured or killed a bishop.[15] At the end of the sixth century (592) St. Gregory reserved to himself the excommunication, with which he threatened Archbishop John of Larissa for having unjustly deposed Adrian, bishop of Thebes. The Council of Limoges (1032 sess. II) imposes the obligation on bishops to send penitents to Rome when in doubt to whom the case be reserved. When Henry IV in the year 1105 asked the legate Richard of Albano to absolve him from the censure of excommunication, the legate replied that the Pope alone could grant absolution in the case.

In the beginning of the twelfth century, the power of the Pope to reserve cases was universally recognized and laws were frequently enacted which evidently implied such jurisdiction. The second Council of the Lateran, 1139 cap. 29, caus. XVIII, quest. IV, by the famous canon of Innocent II (1130-1143), "Si quis suadente diabolo," confirming the Synods of Clermont, 1130, c. 10, Reims 1131, c. 13 and Pisa 1135, decreed that whosoever henceforth laid malicious hand on a cleric or monk, incurred ipso

[10] Wasserschleben, Bussordnung pp. 192 etc.; Canoniste Contemp. 1909 pp. 73 sq. 1915 p. 487 sq.; Londiniensis 1102 cap. 28, Harduin VI., 1866.

[11] Adami Persenniae Abbatis Epist. XXVI. Migne CCXI.

[12] Const. Syn. Odonis Episcopi Paris. circa 1198 cap. VI par. 5 Harduin VI 11, 1940.

[13] St. Thomas in IV Cent. Dist. XIX C. 1. art. 3; Summa Suppli. c. XX art. 2.

[14] Poenit. P Ecberti Liber IV cap. 6.

[15] Cf. c. Synod. Romana 862 or 863. Hefele, I. IV. p. 260; Wernz, tit. VIII no. 164.

facto excommunication, the raising of which, except in danger of death, was reserved to the Pope and had to be sought in person in Rome.[16]

From this time on papal cases became more frequent. To those reserved in the Lateran Council, were added: incendiarism, church-robbery and violation of the enclosure of nuns.[17] The Council of Rouen (Rothomagense) adds perjury, and the Synod of Paris includes simony.[18]

The exact number of cases reserved to the Pope in the twelfth century is not certain. Some authors maintain that there were only two, [19] others three, some as many as six. The Council of Mainz (1261) enumerates only three: violence to clerics, incendiarism and simony. St. Thomas mentions six (Dist. XVIII, Sent. IV, Q. II, art. 5). The Council of Vienne (1311) adds three more to the six reserved before that time. Finally the Council of Constance (1414) instituted a reform movement, the so-called "Collegium Reformatorium" to bring about uniformity.

The steady increase in the number of papal reservations may be ascribed to the growing consciousness of the Church-rights, to the better understanding of the centralized supreme jurisdiction of the Apostolic See, and the increasing facility of communication between Rome and the more distant countries. The ever growing numbers of the faithful coming to Rome from different parts of Europe, to obtain absolution from reserved cases, made it necessary to appoint special priests for this class of penitents. Thus we read that Lucius III (1184) appointed the abbot of Citeaux to absolve incendiaries, fugitive monks and those who communicated in any way with the interdicted. The abbot at first enjoyed this privilege only in regard to those who wished to join the order, but afterwards also in favor of all who chose him as confessor. Pontifical Legates and bishops were endowed with similar faculties and privileges.

The method of procedure and the discipline of reserved cases rendered a permanent office not only useful but necessary. This office gradually developed into the present Tribunal of the Sacred Penitentiaria. Before entering into the subject, a few words in explanation of the pertinent documents are necessary. By an

---

[16] Can. 29 causa 18 q. 4 Lat. II. Pius IX Const. Apost. Sed. no. 2. Phillips, t. I par. 60. Hinchius, t. I p. 118. Wernz, t. VIII no. 164.

[17] Post. Conc. Lat. P XIV c. 2 c. 1, 4, 5, 6, 9, 19, 22, 24. Extr. Lib. VI t. XXXIX.

[18] Conc. Rothomagense, cap. 26. Const. Syn. Odonis Paris. cap. VI par. 6.

[19] Const. Richardi Episc. Sarum a. 1217 cap. 28.

order of Leo XIII the Vatican Archives were opened to truth-seeking investigators, and invaluable material for history was gathered from these sources. Very little regarding the S. Penitentiaria was open for inspection. As a consequence we are still in doubt about the origin and the first constitution. Available documents are incomplete and obscure.

In mode of procedure the S. Penitentiaria undoubtedly followed the custom of the Apostolic Chancery and, like that office, also preserved its formularies and original registers, imposed its taxes and compiled its manuals. We have complete registers of the Chancery from the year 1198. The secret archives alone could give us information in regard to the registers of the S. Penitentiaria. The constitution of Benedict XII (d. 1342) "In agro dominico" does not mention any registers but gives a clear idea of the constitution of this Sacred Agency of Absolution.[20] Even at the time of Eugene IV the registers of the letters and petitions of the S. Penitentiaria were incomplete, because the general rule was to return the petitions to the petitioners. In the Constitution "Prudens paterfamilias" of July 1, 1436, Eugene IV advises, and in a later Constitution of July 11, 1438 he formally decrees, that all letters and petitions of the Sacred Penitentiaria be duly kept on record.[21]

Some extant documents give a more or less clear idea of the original constitution of the Sacred Penitentiaria. There is a manuscript of Cardinal Bentevenga (1279-1289), which contains several documents written by himself, but as he remarks, it is a mere formulary, rather than a method of procedure.[22] One of the most important documents is the so-called "Liber Poenitentiariae," which closely resembles the "Liber Provincialis" of the Chancery. It contains acts of the Penitentiaria and of the Roman Pontiffs relating to the Tribunal. It imposes the obligation on the scribes to procure, within two months after going into office, a copy of the constitution treating on the matter. After these two months have elapsed, the scribes had to acquaint themselves, within the following four months, with the powers of the Major and Minor Penitentiaries, the general and special concessions, the reformed formularies of the Pontiff, the formul-

[20] Denifle. Archiv fur Litt. u. Kirch. Vol. IV. p. 209.

[21] Fondo Vaticano MS. Lat. 3994, f. 88; MS. Lat. 5744 f. 101 v; MS. Reg. Svec. 1796 f. 133 v.

[22] Registerband des Card. Poenitent. Bentevenga. Eubel, Arch. f. kath. Kirchenrecht vol. LXIV 1890 pp. 3-69.

ary of the minor offices and all that was necessary for the exercise of office.[23]

There are three editions of the "Liber Poenitentiariae." The first dates back to the Const. "In agro dominico" of Benedict XII (Apr. 8, 1338) and contains the new tax-list issued by the Pope.[24] One of the MSS points out the "Privileges of the Penitentiaries," another the "Days on which the Penitentiaria is not in session."[25] Another document, "Summa Nicolai" of the year 1291, enumerates the powers and cases reserved to the Major Penitentiary. The second revised edition of the "Liber Poenitentiariae" begins with the Statutes of Benedict XII, and adds the new concessions and reservations with an extract of laws from the Decree of Gratian and Clement V. In it are also recorded the chief offices of the Penitentiaria, the new legislation of Eugene IV and the Statutes of the Major Penitentiary, Jordan Orsini.[26]

Of equal value with the "Liber Poenitentiariae" are the Formularies. These are of great importance, because they help us to understand the mode of procedure in the Sacred Penitentiaria.

The most ancient, it seems, is the "Formae Romanae Curiae compositae a magistro Thomasio bonae memoriae presbytero Cardinali super casibus poenitentiariae."[27] Charles Lea is of the opinion, that Jacobus Thomasius Gaetanus, Cardinal presbyter of St. Clement (1295-1300), composed this formulary, but this is very doubtful. Haskins adduces strong arguments for attributing the formulary to Thomas of Capua, Cardinal priest. This Cardinal held the office of Penitentiary from 1234-1240, during which time the formulary appeared. There is only one form that shows a later date, No. XCI, 2, 1243. Furthermore he is mentioned five times in the Formulary: XXVIII 3, LXIII, 3; LXVI; CXLV 2; CLXXII 7. In the "Salimbene Chronica" (Parma. pp. 66, 194, 1857) he is called the "*Melior dictator de curia*" and in another he is spoken of as the confessor who gives absolution in the

---

[23] Ravenna MS. 470 f. 26 v. Vat. L. Fond. Vat. MS. Lat. 2663 f. 36 v.

[24] MS. Lat. 415 Hofbibliothek Vienna ff. 1-37 (14 cent. 121 ff.). Denifle, Archiv. f. Litt. u., Kirch. des Mittelalters. vol. IV pp. 209 sq.

[25] Vat. Lat. 3994 f. 18 v.; f. 19 and 28 v.

[26] Fondo Vat. MS. Lat. 3994 ff. 83 v-88; 5744 ff. 95-102 v.; 6347 ff. 195-202; MS. Reg. Svec. 1796 ff. 1265-135 v.

The third revision is merely a copy of the second adding the Const. "Provida Romani" of Sixtus IV (Nov. 1, 1437) and ending with the Brief of Julius III (Mar. 1, 1552).

[27] "A Formulary of the Papal Penitentiaria in the thirteenth century," Philadelphia, 1892. It is divided in 355 formulas and 179 rubrics.

place of the Pope (1223).[28] Jacobus Thomasius Gaetanus is never called simply Thomasius, always Jacobus and between the years 1295-1300, Matthias de Aquasparta was Major Penitentiary. If Jacobus Thomisius Gaetanus and not Thomas of Capua is the author of the Formulary, it seems entirely improbable that he would omit all the forms, which were so numerous in his own time, the end of the thirteenth century, and record only those in use fifty years before. All these reasons lead us to conclude, that Thomas of Capua was the author of the famous Formulary.

When Benedict XII April 8, 1338 issued the Constitution "In agro dominico," he not only reconstructed the Curia, but appointed Gaucelinus, bishop of Albano, Gotius, patriarch of Constantinople, Jacobus of Brixen and abbot of the monastery Montisolivi, to reform the original Formulary. It is not altogether certain, whether this reformed Formulary and that of Thomas of Capua are identical. The great similarity between both in regard to matter and form is very striking and apparently there is no doubt that the Formulary of Thomas of Capua at least formed the basis and foundation for the Formulary of Benedict XII.

A short time afterwards Walter of Argenten, scribe and corrector of the Penitentiaria, composed a new Formulary under Urban VI 1389. New concessions granted to the Major Penitentiary and Regent, as well as many new changes made in the old Formulary, are the reasons given by Walter for issuing a new one. This last revision according to three documents, was in use up to the time of Cardinal Calandrini (1476).

[28] Guillaume le Breton Philippeide, XII. II. 721-738 (ed. Delaborde Paris. p. 376). Parma 1851, pp. 66, 194. Canoniste Contemp. Sep. Oct. 1915 Poenitentiaria. Haskins, "The sources for the history of the papal Penit." American Journal of Theology vol. IX. 1905.

CHAPTER II

Constitution of the Sacred Penitentiaria

PART I

After this brief investigation of the historical documents regarding the origin and practices of the Sacred Penitentiaria, we shall treat the Sacred Tribunal as constituted previous to the reformation of Benedict XII in the year 1342.

Benedict XII found "when reading a certain book" that formerly Cardinal Priests assisted the Pope in hearing confessions, and when labors increased in the Roman Curia, Penitentiaries were appointed for the work. In his memorable constitution "In agro dominico" (8 Apr. 1338) he again mentions the fact that Penitentiaries or Archpriests were formerly assistants in the internal forum, with the obligation of hearing confessions and writing the apostolic letters. For composing other acts a librarian and a secretary were employed.

The exact time when the office of the Penitentiary was instituted is not known. As already stated it is not unlikely that it had its origin during the reign of Pope Alexander III (1159-1181). We know that Cardinal John a Sancto Paulo, of the titular Church of St. Pricilla, was appointed by the Pope to hear confessions in his stead: "Quod confessiones pro papa tunc recipiebat" (1193-1205). Apparently he was not the only one to be thus appointed since a letter of Gregory IX mentions the Penitentiary Nicolaus Tusculanus, bishop under Pope Honorius III. It seems at the time of Innocent III this Penitentiary was no longer an ordinary official, but the head of some institution.[1] Under Gregory IX this institution was known by the name of Poenitentiaria. The fact, also that Innocent IV (d. 1254) and Alexander IV (d. 1261) mention the scribes of the Penitentiaria, testifies to the existence of a permanent institution.[2] The earliest letter we have of a Penitentiary, seems to be that of Nicolaus Tusculanus, who had charge of the Penitentiaria during the years 1216-1219. Thomas of Capua the author of the Formulary suc-

[1] Breslau, Urkundenlehre, vol. I, p. 228, n. 2. Pressutti, Regesta Honorii Papae III, index sub Poenitentiarius Chartularium Universitatis Parisiensis, Paris 1889, vol. I, p. 85; Raymundiana pars. II pp. 17 sq.

[2] Breslau, Urkundenlehre, vol. I, p. 228 Potthast, n. 12993.

ceeded him in office (1216-1234).[3] Next in office was Hugo de Sancto Caro (Hugh de St. Cher) cardinal priest of the titular church of St. Sabina (1244-1263). A letter from him of the year 1256, shows that he was the head of the Tribunal during that time. The exact date of his appointment is unknown, but it was probably made under Innocent IV, who entrusted him with various affairs after the Council of Lyons (1245). This cardinal is the first Penitentiary known under the title of Summus or Generalis Poenitentiarius.[4]

Shortly afterwards, under Urban IV (d. 1265), the superior of the Sacred Penitentiary is well known as the Summus Poenitentiarius. The successor of Hugh de St. Cher was Guido Gros, cardinal bishop of Sabina (1261-1265), who afterwards became Pope Clement IV (Feb. 5th, 1265). The immediate successors to the office of Penitentiary are not known, probably because they were appointed temporarily. The next known Grand Penitentiary is Peter of Tarantasia, cardinal bishop of Ostia (1273-1276) afterwards Pope Innocent V (Jan. 21, 1276).[5] Though probably not the immediate successor, Bentevenga, cardinal bishop of Albano, held the office during the years 1278-1289. The Regesta of this Cardinal began in the year 1270. Cardinal Mattheo de Aquasparta of the titular church of St. Lawrence at Damaso (1288-1291), afterwards cardinal bishop of Porto and St. Rufinus (1291-1302), came next in succession. He was a former General of the Franciscans and a renowned theologian. The letters of this Cardinal are quite numerous, as the formularies of the Sacred Penitentiaria show.

Next in office was Gentilis de Montefiore, cardinal priest of San Martino ai Monti (1300-1312); Berengarius Fredoli, bishop of Bézier, afterwards cardinal priest of the Basilica of SS. Nerius and Achilleus, and finally cardinal bishop of Tusculum (d. 1323). Berengarius was one of the collaborators on the Liber Sextus Decretalium under Boniface VIII. Gaucelinus, bishop of Albano, succeeded Berengarius. Gaucelinus was commissioned by Benedict XII to change the old Formulary. He died 1348. Then came Etienne d'Albert (or d'Albret). He was bishop of Noyon 1338, of Clermont 1340, cardinal priest 1342, cardinal bishop of Ostia,

---

[3] Guillaume le Breton Philippeide XII. II. 721-738 ed. Delaborde Paris 1885 p. 376.

[4] The letter of Nicolaus Tusculanus mentions "Summus Poenitentiarius."

[5] Regesta d. Honorius IV, n. 735. Saegmuller, Die Thaetigkeit u. Stellung der Cardinaele bis Papst Bonifaz VIII. Freiburg 1896 pp. 105 sq.

Grand Penitentiary 1352 and finally elected Pope (18 of Dec., 1352). Next in office was Gil de Albornoz the renowned cardinal, general and statesman (d. 23 Aug., 1367). Clement VI created him cardinal priest of San Clemente (17 Dec., 1350). Innocent VI entrusted him with extraordinary powers to restore the authority of the Pope and appointed him legate and Vicar General of the Papal States (30 Jan., 1353). Gil de Albornoz had many substitutes as Grand Penitentiary. Special mention is made of Francis d'Abt, surnamed Florentinus, cardinal priest of St. Mark, and William Bragose, cardinal deacon of St. George at Velabro, afterwards cardinal priest of St. Lawrence at Lucina. Bragose was Grand Penitentiary from 1361-1367. Galhardus de Boscoviridi took charge of the "*regimen curae poenitentiariae*" in 1367.

He was succeeded by Etienne de Poissy, bishop of Paris, cardinal priest of the titular church of St. Eusebius and Grand Penitentiary from 1369-1373. John de Croso, bishop of Limoges, was Penitentiary from 1273-1383.[6] Jead d'Aurelin archbishop of Corfu was elected "regens officii poententiariae" by Pope Urban VI in the year 1378. He afterwards became cardinal priest of Sabina and Grand Penitentiary. The next Penitentiary Eleazar de Sabran, cardinal priest of St. Balbina, was in charge only from Oct. 1378 to Aug. 1378 when he died. Then Augustin de Lanzano, who was not a cardinal, was temporarily appointed. Luc Radulfuci de Gentilibus, cardinal priest of St. Sixtus replaced the former in 1382 and held the position five years. He was succeeded by Ponce de Orvisto after whose death Augustin de Lanzano again took charge. Cardinal Nicholas Mosquino exercised the functions of a Grand Penitentiary a very short time from the 3rd of March to the 29th of July, 1389.

His successor was Francis Corbon cardinal priest of St. Susanna, afterwards bishop of Sabina (1389-1412). Then came Anthony de Cajetanis cardinal priest of St. Cecilia, afterwards bishop of Palestrina and later bishop of Porto. He died 1412.[7] During the Council of Pisa, Gerard and Anthony de Cajetanis were both in office, dividing the work between themselves. Towards the end of the year 1408 John Dominici, cardinal of St. Sixtus, had charge of the Sacred Penitentiaria under Pope Gregory XII. Then followed Jordan de Ursinis, who reigned simultaneously

[6] He was sent to Avignon by Clement VII.

[7] At Avignon we find the following Penitentiaries: John de Crosso, who was sent there by pope Clement VII; Peter Ameli, cardinal priest of St. Mark (d. 1389); Peter Gerard bishop of Puy, cardinal priest of St. Peter in Vinculis (1390) and bishop of Tusculum (d. 1417).

with Peter Gerard from 1415-1438. His successor was Nicholas de Albergatis, cardinal priest of the titular church of the Holy Cross in Jerusalem (d. 9th of May, 1444).

Upon him followed Cesarini, cardinal bishop of Tusculum (d. 1444); John de Capranica, cardinal priest of the titular church of the Holy Cross (d. 1458); Philipp Calendrini, cardinal priest of St. Lawrence at Lucina, afterwards bishop of Albano and Porto (d. 1476); Julian de Revere, Grand Penitentiary from 1476-1503, afterwards Pope Július II; Peter Luigi Borgia, cardinal priest of the titular church St. Marcellus (d. 1511); Leonard Grosso della Revere (d. 1520); Lawrence Pucci (1529) and Anthony Pucci his nephew, cardinal priest and bishop of Sabina (in 1544); Robert Pucci (d. 1547); Ranucci Farnese (d. 1565).

We conclude our list of Penitentiaries with Charles Borromeo, cardinal priest of the titular church of St. Prassede and papal secretary of Pius IV. He resigned his offices as Grand Penitentiary, archbishop of St. Maria Maggiore and other high dignities in the year 1572.

The names we have given and the periods in which these Penitentiaries held office were until quite recently entirely unknown to historians. M. Goeller began the work, and I have verified the data and given the result of his earnest and unbiassed research. When the minds of men will turn from war and carnage and investigation can be peacefully resumed, the old manuscripts yet untouched will no doubt furnish us with still more information especially regarding the organization of the Tribunal and the functions of its various officials. The libraries of the cardinals in charge of the office at various times, will render useful service, as ikewise the original letters, if they can be found, issued by the Penitentiaries. One of the earliest we have is that under seal of Nicholas of Casamari to those who accompanied Louis of France to England.[8]

The work of M. Goeller brings us down to the time of Pope Pius V, who completed the work or reforming the Sacred Penitentiaria, so well begun by Pius IV (d. 1565). Succeeding Popes, as we shall see, took up the task and made new rules and regulations as time and circumstances required, until Pius X by his constitution "Sapienti consilio" (29 June, 1908) gave the Sacred Penitentiaria its present form and powers.

---

[8] Archives Nationales, J. 655, publ. by Teulet, Layettes du Tresor des chartes, Paris 1863 vol. I p. 450 n. 1241; Paston, Geschichte der Paepste vol. I p. 769 n. 1.

PART II

The constitution "In apostolicae" (Apr. 13, 1744) of Benedict XIV with a few exceptions is in full force even at the present time. It confirms the rules laid down by Pius V in the Const. "In omnibus" (June 15, 1569) and gives the number of officials, who constitute the S. Penitentiaria.

According to this constitution the Major Penitentiary must be a cardinal. He must furthermore have the degree of Doctor of Canon Law or be a Licentiate in Theology. He is elected by a Brief of the Pope and must exercise his office in person. If however he is absent for some legitimate reason, approved by the Pope, he can delegate another cardinal with the required qualities, who exercises his office not in the name of the Major Penitentiary, by whom he was delegated, but in his own name.

If the Major Penitentiary dies during the vacancy of the Holy See, a new one is elected by the majority of the cardinals present at the Conclave. This election takes place either in a special meeting before they enter the Conclave, or during the Conclave itself. It is made by a secret vote and the one chosen remains in office only during the time the See is vacant.

Besides the powers of dispensing and absolving, as we shall see when treating of his competency, the Major Penitentiary is chief administrator of the Tribunal. All the other officials are under his jurisdiction and guidance. He may inflict punishment, appoint whom he thinks worthy and exclude the undesirable. He hears confessions of the faithful in the Basilica of St. John at the Lateran on Palm Sunday, in St. Mariae Maioris, on Wednesday of Holy Week, in St. Peter's on Thursday and Good Friday of Holy Week. A special confessional is reserved for this purpose and after each confession he touches the penitent with the so-called penitential rod to which ceremony 100 days of indulgence were attached. By a rescript granted on the 6th of March, 1917, the indulgence has been increased to 300 days.[9] On Ash Wednesday he imposes the ashes on the Holy Father, the cardinals and assistants. He also assists the Pontiff at the hour of death. He solemnly celebrates Mass on All Souls Day in the pontifical chapel. He appoints the Minor Penitentiaries to the Roman Basilicas and the Church of Loreto and grants them the required faculties.[10] He appoints the extraordinary Penitentiaries to St.

[9] Acta Apostolicae Sedis, March, 1917.

[10] Every day they hear confessions in the Basilicas: Lateran, Vatican, Liberiana, the faithful, when touching the penitential rod gain 100 days of indulgences. Acta Ap. Sed. Mar. 1917.

Peter's and during the time of Jubilee to St. Paul's and the other churches of the city. He appoints the assistant, who is delegated to visit the different Penitentiaries to collect the libelli supplices which require special powers and return them to the confessors. He designates priests to conduct the spiritual exercises at the Mission House near the Curia Innocentiana. These exercises are free to all, having been endowed by Vincentius bishop of Preneste and Cardinal Petra.

Benedict XIV allowed the Penitentiary 100 scuta auri (about $100) as monthly salary. 200 scuta from the income of the Penitentiaria were set aside for the poor who had recourse to the Sacred Penitentiary. If the sum did not suffice the Penitentiary was privileged to petition the Holy Father for a greater allowance. Recent laws regarding the Sacred Penitentiaria, have affected many changes and hence some of these powers and privileges have fallen into desuetude.

The Regent, Theologian, Datarius, Canonist, Corrector and Sigillator are elected by the Major Penitentiary. The names of the elected are presented to the Pope for approval and the necessary documents are drawn up. The qualities required of every official are strictly determined. The Regent, Datarius, Theologian and Canonist must be especially acquainted with the various cases of conscience and must be men of superior learning.

The Corrector must be versed in detecting defects and thoroughly acquainted with decrees and formulas pertaining to the Tribunal. The Procurators and Scribes are elected and appointed after a public competitive examination and a searching inquiry by the Regent and Corrector into their lives, morals, age, knowledge and other qualities necessary for such offices. Unless elected in this manner all their concessions, even though for some reason or other made by the Pope himself, are null and void.

Duties of the Regent: By a very old custom the Regent is chosen from among the chaplains of the Pope, one who is an auditor of the Apostolic Curia. It is his duty to examine all cases with the greatest diligence and to direct all negotiations in all sincerity. The Procurator takes all orders from the Regent and can do nothing without his approbation. All matters of minor importance are expedited through the procurator, but any doubtful or difficult case must be referred to the Major Penitentiary, who decides it in the so-called Signatura or congress, a meeting in which the most important cases are discussed.

Duties of the Theologian: For a long time past this official has been chosen from the Society of Jesus. It is his duty to give counsel and advice (in writing if so demanded). All obscure, vague or difficult cases are submitted to the Major Penitentiary.

The Canonist examines the cases proposed to him and gives his decisions either orally or in writing, as the Regent or the Penitentiary may demand.

The Corrector looks over all minutes and petitions drawn up by the Procurators and makes the necessary corrections, so that all letters are expedited in the proper form.

The Datarius affixes the date, the name of the place and the year of the pontificate. Vacancy of the Holy See requires special mention.

The Sigillator or Sealer examines the letters, to see that everything corresponds to the regulations and then adds the seal of the Sacred Penitentiaria. The Sealer is also responsible for the work of any assistant or substitute he may employ.

Each Procurator or Scribe has a particular work assigned him. They examine and classify the letters and petitions sent to the Sacred Penitentiaria. The procurators give them their proper form and then pass them on to the Corrector. The formulas must be approved by the Major Penitentiary and the six officials of the Signatura, and under no consideration can they deviate from the given formulas unless for a grave reason, approved by the Regent or the Penitentiary. The Procurators cannot interfere in giving the final decisions, which depend on the Regent and the Major Penitentiary.

The Scribes or their substitutes compose the letters referred to them in a clear and exact type (formerly in form of a Bull), enter all decrees of the Roman Pontiff, if there are any on the matter, in the respective books and also the instructions or decrees issued by the Major Penitentiary or Signatura. Exceptional cases, special dispensations or extraordinary occurrences are recorded in the same manner.

The number of Procurators and Scribes has not always been the same, Clement V reduced the number to twelve (Sep. 2, 1311. Regesta Clem. Papae V. n. 7359). Before the time of Pius V there were twenty-four Procurators and twenty-seven Scribes. This number was reduced to two Procurators and two Scribes. Benedict XIV again increased the number adding one to each office on account of the additional work. In his Constitution "Quamvis jam" (Dec. 13, 1747) he gave special rules, how these Procurators and Scribes were to be elected and how they were to conduct themselves to acquire the necessary experience. This constitution is still in force in all matters not at variance with the Const.

"Sapienti consilio." The three special rules that govern this Tribunal now are as follows:

1. The Tribunal limited solely to the internal forum retains the following officials: the Cardinal Penitentiary and the Regent, the other five prelates of the Signatura, the Procurator or Secretary, a substitute and some other minor officials.

2. The Tribunal conducts its business according to the forms of the Const. "In apostolicae" (Apr. 13, 1744) excepting those changed afterwards by legitimate custom, which however must be put in writing by the Cardinal Penitentiary and submitted to the Pontiff for approval. The Constitution "Sapienti consilio" and subsequent laws retain their full force.

3. According to the same Const. of Benedict XIV, all business must be transacted gratuitously and with the greatest secrecy (Normae pecul. cap. VIII. art. 1).

The officials of the Sacred Penitentiaria, as mentioned in the official directory, are the following: Datarius, Corrector, Sealer, Canonist, Secretary and Substitute, two Copyists, Secretaries, an Archivist and two Registrars. The Signatura or congress is composed of the Cardinal Penitentiary, Regent, Canonist, Theoogian, Datarius, Sealer, Canonist and Secretary, but the latter has no vote.

According to the Constitution of Benedict XIV, all the offices mentioned are conferred for life, and, excluding the case where an official is legitimately deprived of office, they remain until they voluntarily resign or are raised to the dignity of bishop, cardinal or some higher office in the Penitentiaria. All bargaining for offices is strictly prohibited and unless their lives are beyond reproach, all grants and concessions made to them are null and void.

Only those present are entitled to a salary, unless their absence is unavoidable. If any of the higher officials is legitimately detained, the one next in dignity takes his place as pro N. N. When one of the Secretaries or Copyists is absent, the Major Penitentiary appoints another in his place. The substitutes must all take the oath and are bound by the same obligations as the officials they represent.

Paragraph 25 of the Constitution reads: Since it would not be just that the officiasl, whose work is not light, be deprived of emoluments, we decree that the reimbursements granted them by our predecessors remain in full force. Accordingly the Regent receives 25 scutata monthly, the Datarius, Corrector and Sealer 15, the Theologian and Canonist 10, the Procurators 12, and the

Copyists or Secretaries 6 each. Paper, ink, wax and other accidentals are furnished by the Tribunal.

The Sacred Penitentiaria also employs an administrator. He is obliged to give the required security and manage all finances of the Tribunal according to given norms. He is the custodian of all documents and the registrar of the Sacred Penitentiaria. According to the Constitution of Pius V "In earum rerum commutatione" the Sealer ex officio was the administrator of the Sacred Penitentiaria. Benedict XIV confirmed the ordinance but permitted the Sealer to employ a substitute. This Pro-sealer had to be a cleric and a man whose life was without reproach. All superfluous moneys had to be applied to the Asylum for Poor Invalids, as per Constitution of Innocent XII (June, 1693). The Sealer was then the sole custodian of the sacred archives or the Armarium, but he could permit the Pro-sealer to take charge of the other archives. We are not concerned here with the Minor Penitentiaries, stationed at Rome and elsewhere. It will suffice to mention that they depend entirely on the Major Penitentiary, by whom they are elected and examined. The constitution of Benedict XIV speaks of them also at some length. They have various faculties to absolve, dispense and commute vows, but only within certain limits and under the guidance of the Major Penitentiary.

CHAPTER III

PART I

Competency of the Sacred Penitentiaria

To enumerate the faculties enjoyed by the Sacred Penitentiaria during the first years of its existence is not an easy task. Powers were often granted by word of mouth of which we have no record. More than two centuries after the institution of the Tribunal Eugene IV (d. 1447) wrote: "In regard to the powers of absolution and dispensation, the Sacred Penitentiaria has no firm rules. The concessions are made as circumstances require. Some are in contradiction to others, some are granted only for certain places, others again are uncertain or obscure."

We get some idea of the original faculties of the Sacred Penitentiaria from the writings of Andre'de Escobar, who wrote during the time that Jordanus de Ursinis was Major Penitentiary (1415-1438. He writes: "In short, my Lord, Father Jordanus de Ursinis, bishop of Albano, in virtue of the Constitution of Benedict XII, can dispense from every sin and crime against the canons and decrees of the Roman Pontiff, from every major or miner excommunication, especially from the major, from suspension, interdict and irregularity. He can dispense from every irregularity contracted either knowingly or ignorantly as long as it is not of the divine law or contrary to the apostolic rule or not especially and nominally reserved to the Pope, or promulgated ab homine or the Apostolic See."

It was the privilege of the Major Penitentiary to hear confessions of the cardinals, patriarchs, bishops and abbots. He presided over the Minor Penitentiaries, when they inflicted punishments or he mitigated excessive penalties. Special cases and enormous crimes were referred to him alone. The canonist John of God sums up his powers in these words: "Quia postquam gerit papae vices, ergo personam in poenitentiis representat." At the time of the Council of Lyons (1244) he alone could absolve the officials of the Curia from excommunication incurred for simony, except in danger of death, when every priest can absolve. The Constitution "Saepe contingit" of Clement IV (d. 1268) grants him the privilege of absolving the bishops of Italy from suspension inflicted for ordaining clerics without the permission of the Pope or their ordinaries. Gradually he was authorized to grant indults and privileges, to give permission to choose confessors, grant indulgences, commute vows, to give absolutions and dispensations.

After the time of Innocent VI (d. 1362), formerly a Grand Penitentiary (Etienne Aubert), the Major Penitentiary regularly received the power to absolve "*a sententiis latis in die Jovis sancta.*" The different faculties, which it would be useless to mention, can be found in the various constitutions as: "Saepe contingit" (Clement IV d. 1268); "De advocatis" (Gregory X d. 1276); "Proinde accedentis" and "Episcoporum" (Boniface VIII d. 1303); "Antiquae" (John XXII d. 1334); "In agro dominico," "Vas electionis" (Benedict XII d. 1342) and "Ne in vinea" (Urban V d. 1370). According to these constitutions the Major Penitentiary can absolve from simony, homicide and mutilation, from violence to clerics, heresy and schism. He can absolve those who have falsified or abused the papal letters, but in regard to the latter only in minor cases, since the more important ones were reserved to the Pope.

1. *Dispensations:* The Penitentiaria dispenses from irregularities ex corpore vitiato and ex defectu natalium. In virtue of the faculties granted by Gregory X (d. 1276) the Penitentiary could dispense "without letters and witnesses for the internal forum, those who contracted marriage in the fourth degree of affinity unaware of the impediment, but only when the impediment was an occult one." Clement VI (d. 1352) granted the power to dispense from the impediment of the fourth degree of consanguinity and affinity, if the marriage had been contracted and the parties were ignorant of such impediments. Gregory XI granted the privilege to the Major Penitentiary to dispense in cases of the fourth degree of consanguinity arising from the impediment of public decency, if the marriage was contracted in ignorance of the impediment and the publication of banns had taken place.

Alexander V (d. 1410) permitted the Penitentiary to dispense from the impediment of consanguinity and affinity in the third degree both for marriages to be contracted and marriages already contracted, but only under certain conditions. At the further request of the Penitentiary, that he be given the power to dispense also from the impediment of spiritual relationship, the request was granted only for those marriages contracted in ignorance of said impediment. Eugene IV (d. 1447) retracted the privilege of dispensing from the impediment of the third degree but gave permission to dispense from the impediment of the fourth degree of consanguinity and affinity for marriages to be contracted.

2. *Commutation of vows:* In the thirteenth century even the Minor Penitentiaries had the privilege of commuting vows, of extending the time for their fulfillment and of reducing the penalty for breaking them. Nicholas IV in his "Summa de absolutionibus et dispensationibus" (1290) reserved the following to the Major Penitentiary: Vow of religion, the vow of continency, the vows of visit the Holy Places, St. Peter's and St. Paul's and St. James' at Compostella.

Gregory XI (d. 1378) authorized the Penitentiary to dispense from the vows of visiting the Holy Sepulchre and other oversea places under certain conditions i. e. all proceeds were to be applied to the fabrics of St. Peter's and St. Paul's. Under Sixtus IV commutation of vows to visit Rome or Compostella was not only granted in favor of women but to all in general.

3. *Special powers of the Major Penitentiary:* In some cases the Major Penitentiary enjoyed the same powers as the bishops. Benedict XII permitted them to grant *"de gratiis quae conceduntur episcopis,"* to absolve and dispense *"ad certum numerum"* as is granted to bishops. The Tribunal was privileged to reconcile apostates, especially "apostatae a religione," and to grant ecclesiastical burial to those excommunicated.

Benedict XII gives a twofold series of faculties enjoyed by the Sacred Penitentiary: the ordinary faculties and the special faculties. Later a third series embracing the cases, which demanded a special indult of the Holy Father was added. Thus the Council of Constance states: "the power of the Major Penitentiary is threefold: the first is the ordinary, the second is that by which he dispenses in cases requiring special faculties and the third, where a special power is granted him by the Pope for exceptional cases."

The Bull "In apostolicae" of Eugene IV formed the basis of the powers of the Sacred Penitentiaria in the fifteenth century. It eliminated the superfluous grants and issued new faculties and privileges, but in a precise and definite manner, forbidding any one to exceed these powers without a special permission of the Pope. Nicholas V, Calistus II, Paul II, again made some changes as circumstances demanded. Sixtus IV in the year 1484 gave explicit and specific rules for the new concessions.

Under Clement VII (d. 1543), when the Sacred Penitentiaria had full sway and apparently was at the height of its power, new reformatory laws were introduced. The Major Penitentiary, who up to this time exercised full powers, both in the internal and in the external forum and was unhampered in granting decisions on innumerable matters, was obliged to abide by the new ordinances. With the consent of the Pope, Anthony Pucci ordained that the chief members of the Penitentiaria meet with the Cardinal Penitentiary weekly and discuss all important matters at the so-called Signatura or congress. The laws enacted up to the end of the fifteenth century in regard to the Sacred Penitentiaria clearly show that its powers extended not only to the internal forum but to the external as well. It is certain that in the thirteenth century, the Major Penitentiary exercised his powers for both forums. He dispensed from ecclesiastical impediments, legitimated children, absolved from homicide, granted permission to acquire benefices, dispensed from the defect of age or body for the reception of Holy Orders and granted indulgences. This shows how the Sacred Penitentiaria had gradually drifted away from its original institution and had exceeded all faculties, which it originally enjoyed. Sixtus IV in his constitution "Quoniam Nonnulli" (May —th, 1484) mad this clear, when he stated: "It is said that the powers of the Sacred Penitentiaria extend only to the forum of conscience and that it cannot grant the apostolic powers, which it enjoys to others." To remove all doubts it was decreed that the Sacred Tribunal can delegate its powers and that all its rescripts have full force in both forums.

This encroachment upon the powers and faculties of other congregations soon proved undesirable, and laws were enacted to restrict and define the privileges and rights of the Tribunal. Julius III and Pius IV deprived it of all rights to commute the last wills of the faithful, to suppress or transfer benefices, to admit voluntary homicides to major Orders, to permit religious to remain outside of their monasteries and to concede matrimonial dispensations in forma gratiosa.

Pius IV in his Constitution "In sublimi" (May 4th, 1562), though he did not deprive the Tribunal of all juridical power in the external forum, imposed upon it certain conditions and limitations.

Leo X continued this reform movement. His Constitution "Pastoralis officii" (Dec. 13th, 1513) commands the Correctors and Auditors of the Sacred Penitentiaria to admit no scandalous, unusual, or inappropriate cases, and to observe under pain of excommunication the rules and modifications made regarding the taxes. Procurators should be satisfied with half the tax and ask no more than is necessary to exedite letters and rescripts.

Pius V in his Constitution "In omnibus" (May 18th, 1569) proceeds with still greater severity. He says, "Since human weakness and negligence have corrupted many, all previous powers of the Sacred Penitentiaria are recalled." The new faculties granted by him were to be interpreted strictly and used conscientiously. "We demand that this be observed in the most holy and inviolable manner, namely that nothing be asked for composing or expediting letters, nothing for paper, ink, seal, cover, cords and other things pertaining to the sending of letters." In another constitution "Ut bonus paterfamilias" (May 18th, 1569) he demands that henceforth only those faculties are to be granted, which serve as real remedies to the faithful and are proper to the penitential office of the Tribunal. The same zeal for reform actuated Pope Urban VIII, when he issued his Constitution "Regimini" (June 10th, 1634). The Bulls "Romanus Pontifex (Sep., 1682) of Innocent XII and "Apostolatus Officii" (Oct., 1732) of Clement XIII merely confirm these restrictions made by their predecessors.

Thus the Sacred Penitentiaria was restricted to the forum of conscience, its office was well determined and the qualities of the various officials specified. The Tribunal became a true dispenser of spiritual remedies.

Benedict XIV in his masterly way continued the reform and wrote the four constitutions: "In apostolicae" (Apr. 13th, 1744); "Pastor bonus" of the same date; "Quamvis jam" (Dec. 13th, 1747); "Pastoralis" (Aug. 5th, 1748). Restricted and guided by these various ordinances the Sacred Penitentiaria dispensed its graces without hampering any other ecclesiastical organization.

The Dataria, it is true, was entirely impeded in the exercise of its functions on account of the civil disturbances of the eighteenth century, and the Sacred Penitentiaria through necessity granted almost all dispensations. When the civil affairs adjusted themselves the Dataria was reinstated in its former office of dispensing in the external forum, but with this restriction that the Sacred Penitentiaria should retain the power of dispensing the poor or quasi poor in both forums. Spain and Portugal however were exempted from the jurisdiction of the Sacred Penitentiaria. This extraordinary faculty of dispensing the poor and the quasi poor was the cause of long disputes between the Dataria and the Sacred Penitentiaria. This dispute was decided in the following manner. To the question: "Do the new rules made by the Dataria apply to the dispensations granted by the Penitentiaria," the S. Tribunal gave the following answer: "In the practice of the Sacred Penitentiaria no innovation has been made" (July 23, 1902). This reply was confirmed on Jan. 2nd, 1904.[1]

With the additional faculties received during the French revolution the Sacred Penitentiaria kept all its powers intact from the time of Benedict XIV to the latest constitution of Pius X, "Sapienti consilio" (June 29th, 1908). Henceforth the Sacred Penitentiaria is limited to the forum of conscience. No doubt Pius X, when making the change, had in mind the constitution "In eligendis" (Oct. 9, 1562) of Pius IV, according to which the Major Penitentiary and his officials can act only in the forum of conscience. In all other matters, with the exception of indulgences the Sacred Tribunal is powerless and its acts null and void.

PART II

Indulgences

Once admitted that the Church has the power to forgive sins, the power of granting indulgences is logically inferred. If the Sacraments of the Church can free one from guilt and eternal punishment, it plainly follows that the Church can also free him from the lesser or temporal punishment. Our Lord said to St. Peter: "I will give to thee the keys of the kingdom of heaven, and whatever thou shalt bind upon earth shall be bound also in heaven, and whatever thou shalt loose upon earth shall be loosed also in heaven" Matt. xvi, 19; xviii, 18. That this power, as the Council of Trent shows, was exercised from the earliest times, is shown by St. Paul in his letter to the Corinthians (II. Cor. ii, 5-10). St. Paul had bound the guilty Corinthian with the fetters of excommunication, he releases the penitent from this penalty by exercising his authority in the person of Christ.

Every Christian knows, that, even though sin is remitted, the temporal punishment due to sin might still remain (II Kings xii, 13; Gen. iii, 17; Ex. 32, 14, 27; Num. xx, 2). How does the Church exercise the God-given power to remit the temporal punishment? An essential element in indulgences is the application of the satisfaction performed by Christ and His Saints to others. Merit is personal and cannot be transferred; satisfac-

[1] Praxis apostolicarum dispensationum super impedimentis matrimonialibus in Dataria Apostolica. No. 206.

tion can be applied to others. This tranfer is based on the Communion of Saints. "We being many, are one body in Christ, and every one members of another" (Rom. xii, 5). It is secondly based on the principle of vicarious satisfaction (Coll, i, 24). Thirdly it is based on the treasury of the Church (I. Jo. ii, 2). "All the Saints intended that whatever they did or suffered for God's sake, should be profitable not only to themselves but to the whole Church."[1]

Hence the practice of granting indulgences, whereby the Church comes to the penitent's assistance and places at his disposal the treasury of the merits of Christ and His Saints. Though closely connected with penance, indulgences are not a part of the Sacrament, they presuppose Confession and Absolution and are properly called an extra-sacramental remission of the temporal punishment incurred by sin.

The indulgences granted by the S. Penitentiaria, like absolution and dispensations, have been the object of bitter accusations. History records some writs containing indulgences from guilt and punishment (a culpa et a poena) and these are the source of great misunderstandings.[2] Some authors as Nicolas of Cusa in the fifteenth century, affirm that the Church at one time granted a dispensation from Confession. Clement V (d. 1314) condemned the practice of these purveyors of indulgences, who pretended to absolve from guilt and punishment.[3] The Council of Constance (1414) revoked all indulgences containing the said formula (Sess XLII n. 14). Benedict XIV (d. 1758) treated these indulgences as spurious and ascribed them to the illicit practice of the "questores" or purveyors.[4]

What is the maning of the formula "a culpa et a poena" and the more or less equivalent formulas as "poenitentiam levamus et remissionem peccatorum facimus," "peccatorum veniam pollicemus"?

H. C. Lea claims that such formulas have been in use in the Church as early as the eleventh century or ever earlier. Enemies of the Church have distorted the doctrine of Christ. Either through ignorance or malice, they have gone so far as to accuse the Church of granting pardon for future sins.[5] The true mean-

[1] Alexander Hales, Summa IV, Q. XXIII. m. 3, n. 6; Albertus Magnus, IV Sent. dist. XX art. 16; St. Thomas, IV Sent. dist. XX Q. I art. 3 sol. 1; Quod lib. II Q. VII art. 16; Cath. Ency. Penance. Indulgences.

[2] Pesch, Theol. Dogm. VII 196, par. 464; Lea, Hist. III, 54; Beringer, Les Indulg. t. I p. 14.

[3] Clem. IV tit. 9, c. 11.

[4] De synod. dioc. VIII, v. 117.

[5] Schiller, Mary Stuart.

ing of the formulas, which have been the occasion of so much controversy, is that indulgences presuppose the Sacrament of Penance and that the penitent is freed from temporal punishment only after sacramental absolution from the guilt of sin has been granted.[6]

No one denies that mercenary members of the flock have been guilty of grave abuses to fill their purses. Martin V in his Bull "Inter cunctas" (Denz. n. 57) writes "Utrum credat, quod Papa omnibus Christianis vere contritis et confessis ex causa pia et justa possit concedere indulgentias in remissionem omnium peccatorum (Clem. V. t. 9. c. 2). Cum aliqui ex ipsis (questoribus) eos a poena et a culpa, ut eorum verbis utamur absolvant, nos, abusus hujusmodi . . . omnimodo abolere volentes" etc.

History proves that, excepting a small minority, the greater number of Catholics have never misunderstood these formulas.[7] Why not reasonably believe that the majority of the people in the Middle Ages thought about the matter as we do, and understood peccatum here as meaning, poena peccati and not culpa, which can be remitted only by the Sacrament of Penance? St. Peter interprets peccatum in that way when speaking of our Lord. "Who His ownself bore our sins in His body upon the tree" (I Pet. 2, 24; Is. 53, 5). Why should they not understand that, where an indulgence is granted in connection with the "*litterae confessionales*," peccatum means culpa, which is forgiven by absolution, whereas temporal punishment is condoned by the indulgences?

We fully appreciate the fact that the study regarding these formulas must be carried on, not only in the field of exegesis, but also from the historical point of view. Earnest endeavors have been made in the last few years in this regard and valuable documents have been discovered. M. Goeller has made a careful research into this matter, and his explanation no doubt will meet with the approval here, as it did with the learned in Germany and France. He claims that the solution of the difficulty is found in the right interpretation of the so-called "*confessionalia*" or "*litterae confessionales.*" These letters were granted either by the bishop or the Pope and gave the holder the right to choose his own confessor, aside from the one which the law prescribed for him.

[6] Bellarmine, De Indulg. I, 7.

[7] A. Franz, Wie man dem Volke im 15 Jahr, uber den Ablass predigte. Katholik, 1904 II 115. Beringer, die Ablasse 12 Aufl S. 12 Paderborn, 1900; Pohle Lehre der Dogmatik B. III S. 508.

Previous to this concession, the pastor alone had the right to hear the confessions of his parishioners.

These "*litterae confessionales*," which left the faithful free to choose their own confessor, were granted as early as the thirteenth century, and as the documents show, this choosing of one's confessor, was then quite prevalent. The Formulary of Thomasius contains letters of the Sacred Penitentiaria granting this "*facultas eligendi confessorem*." A century later we frequently encounter these privileges of choosing a confessor, who could grant "*plena remissio omnium peccatorum*" to the dying.

The development was of course a gradual one. At first it was a simple permission of choosing a confessor. Very soon the chosen confessor received the power to absolve from all sins that were not reserved to the Pope. A little later the same powers were given with the addition of granting particular favors. Finally general faculties were granted to these confessors to absolve from all sins, even those reserved to the Pope.

Clement V granted the indult to Mary of France (1306): "eligere sibi confessorem, qui eam absolvere valeat etiam a quibuscumque sententiis, sacrum ei ministrare et dispensare super observantia jejuniorum." John XXII granted her the same favor "eligere confessorem cui conceditur facultas eam absolvendi in omnibus casibus etiam episcopis reservatis et ab excommunicationis sententiis a canone promulgatis, si quas incurrerit, nisi talia fuerint propter quas sedes apostolica esset merito consulenda." On the 17th of April, 1318, Bishop Arnold of Lombez received from John XXII the privilege to choose his confessor, to whom the power would be given to absolve him from an irregularity reserved to the Major Penitentiary. During the time of Clement VI the formula "eligere confessorem, qui absolvere valeat a casibus Sedi apostolicae reservatis" was commonly employed.

In speaking of the more important formulas, which bring us closest to the point in question, we note the following. Among the *litterae confessionales*, which John XXII granted in the last few years of his pontificate, we find one that reads: "ut confessor tuus, quem duxeris eligendum, omnium peccatorum, de quibus corde contritus et ore confessus exstiteris, ac poenarum etiam quibus tunc pro peccatis ipsis eris obnoxius, eam plenam remissionem, quam Romani Pontifices consueverunt per speciale privilegium aliquibus impertire, quatenus claves Ecclesiae se extendunt et gratum in oculis maiestatis divinae fuerit, in mortis articulo tibi auctoritate nostra concedere valeat, tenore praesentium concedimus facultatem." We have here in the language of the times, a full remission from all sins and penalties. (*Plena remissio omnium peccatorum.*) Without the least modification of the power, a slight change of terms gives us the celebrated formula: indulgentia *a culpa et a poena.*

In the confessional letters granted to Philip V, king of France, and Joanna his wife, the terms are identical. "Mandamus quatenus ei regenti, criminum suorum, de quibus corde contritus et ore confessus infra unius anni spatium fuerit, plenam semel indulgeas veniam peccatorum, illaque sibi auctoritate nostra plena remittas, et quatenus claves Ecclesiae se extendunt et gratum in oculis divinae maiestatis fuerit, satisfactionem impendendam, ut debite satisfaciat, eidem injungas."

Another concession granted to Clementine the Queen of Louis le Hutin, Philip's brother, contains the same privilege, absolutio et indulgentia a poena et a culpa." Many more could be cited from the fourteenth century. One of 1343 reads: "Te placeat plenissimam indulgentiam, quae vulgariter a poena dicitur et a culpa, in mortis articulo eidem Guidoni et Amebae uxori suae concedere ut in forma Fiat," etc. Another: "Suplicat S. V. Bartholomaeum de Thomasiis ut a poena et a culpa et etiam ab excommunicatione et irregularitate eundem absolvere dignemini."

The formula of absolution for the dying, with full remission from sin and punishment, removes the last vestige of daubt. "Primo ipse absolvendus dicat litteraliter vel vulgariter: Confiteor Deo. . . . Et si dicere non potest, dicat alius vice ejus. Quo dicto, sacerdos qui eium absolvere debet dicat Misereatur, et postea subjungat sic dicens: Ego auctoritate Dei, beatorum Petri et Pauli ac aliorum apostolorum omniumque sanctorum et sanctarum Dei et auctoritate d. Urbani papae quinti, qua fungor, mihi in hoc casu specialiter et expresse commissa, absolvo te ab omni vinculo excommunicationis generaliter vel specialiter latae ab homine vel a canone et ab omni vinculo seu poena irregularitatis, suspensionis vel cujuscumque senten etiae, quam scienter vel ignoranter incurristi usgue in hanc horam a judice vel a jure, et restituo te unitati fidelium Christi et sanctis sacramentis Ecclesiae in nomine P. et F. et Sp. S. Amen.

Item eadem auctoritate Dei et Ejus vicarii domini Urbani papae V mihi in hoc casu expresse commissa, absolvo te ab omnibus peccatis tuis, de quibus contritus es corde et ore confessus specialiter vel communiter pro modulo tuae fragilitatis, ac etiam de quibus oblitus es in speciali conteri vel confiteri, et ab omnibus poenis tibi debittis pro tuis peccatis quantum se extendit potestas clavium beatissimi apostoli Petri vicarii Dei in nomine Patris etc."

To sum up the arguments we find that "*indulgentia a poena et a culpa*" is the equivalent of "remissio omnium culparum et poenarum." These formulas employed by the Holy See empowered the holder to select his own confessor, who absolved him from sin and granted him the indulgence. These faculties, namely to absolve from sin and grant the indulgence, embraced in the one formula, are called, "indulgentia a culpa et a poena." Our concept of indulgences is restricted to the remission of temporal punishment and presupposes the absolution from sin. The whole difficulty in the past resulted from confounding the terms indulgentia a culpa et a poena, with the theological concept we have of indulgences.[8]

While it cannot be denied, that abuses were widespread, it must also be remembered that, even when corruption was at its worst, these spiritual grants were being used properly by the sincere members of the laity, who sought them in the right spirit, and by the priests and preachers, who took care to insist on the need of true repentance. For this reason the Church instead of abolishing them, aimed rather at confirming the practice, by the elimination of abuses.

The Council of Trent, after deploring the fact, that in spite of the remedies prescribed by earlier councils, the traders in indulgences continued their nefarious practice, ordained that purveyors be entirely eliminated and the indulgences be henceforth published by the bishop gratuitously, so that all may understand that spiritual treasures are dispensed only for the sake of piety and not of lucre (Sess XXI, c. ix). In the year 1567 St. Pius V cancelled all grants of indulgences involving any fees or financial transactions. Since that time the Church has frequently reiterate her doctrine, to separate the chaff from the wheat, to denounce abuse and enforce her ordinances. Canon 2327 in the New Code reads: Questum facientes x indulgentiis plectuntur ipso facto excommunication Sedi Apostolicae simpliciter reservata. The New Code hereby confirmed the sanction contained in the Constitution of Pius IX "Apostolicae Sedis" (ser. 2, n. II) and in the decree of Pius IV "Romanum decet Pontificem" (7th of Nov., 1562).

---

[8] For a more detailed account see M. Goeller; A. Villien in Le Canoniste Contemporain 1915, p. 583. Also Simony in the Christian Church by Rev. N. A. Weber, S. M., S. T. D. Green, Indulgences, Sacramental Absolution and the Tax Tables of the Roman Chancery and Penitentiaria.

Up to the time of Clement VIII, the Sacred Penitentiaria was competent in all things pertaining to indulgences. Clement VII instituted a special Congregation for Indulgences, and Clement IX in his Bull "In ipsis Pontificatus nostri primordiis" (July 6, 1669) gave the Congregation its definite shape and form. The competencey of this new congregation consisted in "solving all doubts and difficulties regarding relics and indulgences," but it could give no dogmatic decisions in the matter. In the course of time the congregation was endowed with numerous powers and privileges. It was reorganized by Clement XI, 1710.

By a Motu proprio of Pius X "Quae in Ecclesia" (Jan. 28, 1904) the Congregation of Indulgences was united with the Congregation of Rites. In the Constitution "Sapienti consilio" all matter pertaining to the doctrine and the use of indulgences, was committed to the Holy Office, everything concerning relics was transferred to the Congregation of Rites. Benedict XV, by a Motu proprio "Alloquentes proxime" (Mar. 25, 1917), suppressed the Congregation of the Index and committed its ministries to the Holy Office. In order not to burden the Holy Office with too much work, all matters concerning the concessions and the use of indulgences are again committed to the Sacred Penitentiaria. The Holy Father reserved everything concerning the Dogma of new prayers and devotions to the Holy Office, "salvo jure S. Officii videndi ea quae doctrinam circa novas orationes et devotiones respiciunt."

Hence under the Pope the Sacred Penitentiaria has supreme authority in granting indulgences, solving difficulties or answering questions regarding them. According to an instruction of the S. C. of Indulgences Jan. 28, 1756 (9 n. 205. 371) all general concessions granted by the Pope were invalid unless a copy of these indulgences was sent to said Congregation.[9] The New Code can. 920 decrees: "Those who have asked the Roman Pontiff for concessions of indulgences for all the faithful, are obliged, under pain of nullity, to send an authentic copy of the granted indulgences to the Sacred Penitentiaria."

"New indulgence, according to canon 919, also those granted to Churches of Regulars, which are not promulgated in Rome, cannot be published without consulting the Ordinary." "Books of indulgences, summaries, pamphlets, leaflets etc. containing concessions should not be published without the permission of

[9] Decretum S. C. Indulg. April 14, 1856; Dec. 15, 1859; Norma peccul. c. VII, art. 1 no. 8.

the Ordinary of the place." An express permission of the Apostolic See is required to publish in any language authentic collections of prayers or pius works to which the Apostolic See has attached indulgences, or catalogues of Apostolic Indulgences, or summaries of indulgegences either previously collected and never approved or now for the first time collected from various concessians" Can. 1388 par. 1, 2.

An official publication of indulgences was made by Pope Leo XIII in the year 1883 (Decretum authenticum) and contains the decisions of the S. C. of Indulgences from the years 1668-1882. The work "Raccolta di orazioni e pie opere le quale sono state concesse dai Sommi Pontefici le SS. Indulgenze" is authentic and enjoys full authority. The last edition appeared in 1898 and is prefaced by the decree of the S. C. of Indulgences (July 23, 1898).[10]

PART III

Competency of the Sacred Penitentiaria According to the Constitution "Sapienti Consilio" and the New Code

"The jurisdiction of this tribunal of justice," says the decree "Sapienti consilio" and the New Code in like terms, "is limited solely to those matters, which regard the internal sacramental and non-sacramental forum. The power to dispense from matrimonial impediments in the external forum having been transferred to the Congregation of the discipline of the Sacraments, this tribunal grants graces, absolutions, dispensations, commutations, ratifications and condonations. It deals also with questions of conscience and renders decisions regarding same."

Canon 258 of the New Code reads practically the same way. The second paragraph of this canon adds the new faculties acquire by the Sacred Tribunal in virtue of the Motu proprio "Alloquentes proxime" (Mar. 25, 1917). It reads; "Moreover it is its office to judge about all things that pertain to the use and concession of indulgences; the right of the Holy Office regarding dogmatic doctrine about these same indulgences or new prayers and devotions remaining intact."

---

[10] F. M. Cappello, Curia Rom. Sede plena. pp. 67 sq.; Noldin, n. 314 sq.; Santi, lib. V p. 35. Boudinhon. Sur l'histoire des indulgences à propos d'un livre rècent Lea in Revue d'histoire et de litt. relig. III 1898; Baumgarten, Leo's Historical Writings, N. Y., 1909; Rescripta authentica, by Joseph Schneider, Ratisbon 1885.

We notice at first glance how extensive the powers of the Sacred Penitentiaria are in the internal forum. "In a certain sense," writes F. M. Capello, "its faculties are universal regarding persons, places and even matters to some degree." It grants graces, dispenses, and gives decisions from which there is no appeal. It has supreme competency because it receives it immediately from the Pope himself.[1]

Innocent XII, in his Constitution "Romanus Pontifex" (3 Non. Sep., 1682), and Clement XII, in his Const. "Apostolatus Officium" (Non. Oct., 1732), and lastly Benedict XIV, in the Const. "Pastor bonus," catalogued and determined its faculties. The Const. "Pastor bonus" remains in full force in all that is not at variance with the law of Pius X. Only in extraordinary cases the Sacred Penitentiaria is limited in its jurisdiction, but as Benedict XIV says: "Salva semper Maioris Poenitentiarii facultate R. Pontificem consulendi in quibus particularibus casibus etiam per praesentes litteras non concessis imo prohibitis, seu reservatis et exceptis."

The sphere of the Sacred Penitentiaria henceforth is the internal forum alone. Even here some restrictions must be kept in mind. The Sacred Congr. of the Holy Office dispenses from the impediments of mixed religion and disparity of worship. The Holy Office has exclusive rights in regard to the Pauline privilege and deals with all matters which, directly or indirectly, concern faith and morals; it judges heresy and all offences that lead to the suspicion of heresy (Capello vol. I. pp. 63, 79).

The Sacred Penitentiaria therefore dispenses in occult case, or in other words, it dispenses in all cases that are not of the external forum. It absolves not only in occult cases but also in public cases. the reason of this important difference is: absolution belongs to the forum of conscience in which the Sacred Tribunal is alone competent. Another distinction is to be noted, that in occult cases the Sacred Penitentiaria absolves through the aid of the confessor and in public cases only through the intervention of the Ordinary.[2]

It is important to bear in mind, what is meant by the forum of conscience, which is either sacramental or extra-sacramental. The Sacred Tribunal is competent in both, either through the ordinary jurisdiction, which it enjoys or the extraordinary faculties,

---

[1] F. M. Capello, De Curia Rom. Sede Plena. Rome 1911 p. 357.

[2] Capello, De Curia Rom. vol. I p. 356.

which it may easily obtain. The Forum says Ojetti is twofold; the ecclesiastical or civil forum.[3] The ecclesiastical forum is again subdivided into the external or the internal forum. The external forum refers to the public good of the faithful, or in other words, is concerned with the whole corporate body of the Church. The internal forum regards the private good of the individual. The jurisdiction of the internal forum deals therefore with questions concerning the welfare of the individual Christians and with their relations to God. Hence it is also called the forum of conscience. The internal forum is again divided into the sacramental or penitential forum and into the extra-penitential forum.

Cases concerning the private and secret needs of the faithful, can often be expedited outside of the sacramental confession. Thus for instance the Sacred Penitentiaria absolves from vows and secret censures and dispenses from occult impediments. Suarez writes: Guilt requires absolution in the forum of conscience (sacramental forum) but penalty and censures can be removed outside of confession (extra-sacramental forum). "The confessor" says Bonacina, "who has the faculty to absolve in the tribunal of penance, can absolve outside of sacramental confession, when the pardon is asked for matters that do not require sacramental absolution, unless the words of the rescript demand otherwise."[4]

Bearing these distinctions in mind, we proceed to enumerate the powers of the Sacred Penitentiaria as contained in the Constitution "Pastor bonus."

1. The Sacred Penitentiaria absolves from sins and censures any person of any degree or dignity, ecclesiastics or seculars, of any order, congregation, society or institute, all regulars or lay-persons of either sex. It absolves from every guilt, crime or excess no matter how grievous or atrocious, be they public or occult, in whatever way they have been perpetrated or committed, from all excommunications and suspensions or interdicts, and from censures and ecclesiastical punishments imposed and inflicted for such crimes.

It absolves not only in cases reserved to the Ordinaries and superiors of religious, but also from those reserved in a special manner to the Pope and the Holy See and also from those reserved by special letters issued yearly on Holy Thursday. A

[3] Ojetti, Synopsis Rerum. Forum.

[4] Bonacina, De censuris disp. I q. 3, p. 6, n. 8.

salutary penance according to the nature of the guilt must be always imposed and all that the laws require must be observed.

It absolves in both forums secular, ecclesiastic and lay-persons: (1) from censures imposed by law, especially those reserved to the Apostolic See, even when individually mentioned; (2) from censures inflicted nominatim ab homine: (a) when the jurisdiction of the author of the censures has expired; (b) when the absolution is reserved to the Roman Pontiff or the Holy See; (c) when the persons censured are legitimately hindered to appear before those who censured them or those appointed by law. To this norm the constitution adds: "The penitents must abide by the decision and satisfy all claims of a third party."

Pilgrims coming to Rome are absolved from censures to gain the indulgences but with the sanction "cum reincidentia" unless the necessary conditions have been fulfilled. It absolves from occult heresy even when some external acts have been committed, provided that they are not public. Public heretics are absolved in the forum of conscience when no denunciation of occomplices is required. It dispenses from irregularities and inhability "ex quocumque delicto et defectu," except voluntary homicide and other grave excesses. It absolves secular heretics or apostates from irregularity and infamy, when their crime is a secret one, and grants them permission to receive Holy Orders and accept benefices. It grants homicides, exiled and other criminals the privilege to join a religious order and make the profession, provided they do not receive any Orders during their Novitiate. It absolves in occult cases those who fraudulently have been promoted to any Orders. Monitis monendis, it absolves in occult cases those, who have received Orders by committing simony conjointly with the bishop. It revalidates the titles of benefices which have been obtained by some occult crime or vice.

2. *Condonations:* The constitution admonishes the Sacred Penitentiaria to abstain from condoning simoniacal money taken from the Church or the poor, unless the perpetrators are poor themselves, in which case all that remains must be returned to those, who have been unlawfully deprived thereof. In occult cases it condones the fruits received by default, grants faculties to condone goods unjustly acquired, if quality or necessity warrants it, otherwise with the clause: to restore to the poor or the places despoiled.

It permits virgins or even non-virgins to enter a monastery without an inheritance. It absolves from all oaths, when the absolution does not violate the rights of a third party.

3. *Commutations:* It dispenses from or commutes simple vows even though they be reserved or confirmed by oath. In dispensing from the vow of chastity it also grants permission to contract matrimony.

4. *Dispensations:* It dispenses from or commutes the recitation of canonical hours. It dispenses the religious from irregularity incurred "ex defectu vel delicto," either for Orders received or those to be received. It grants them privileges, permits them to retain their offices or benefices, religious dignities and the exercise of their rights. This however has no general application, when it is question of a public defectus natalium. It dispenses religious apostates or fugitives, but only after their superiors have been notified and under pain of relapsing into the same censure, if they do not return. With the permission of the superiors, it can allow a religious, for just reasons, to join a more lenient order. It dispenses nuns from censures, defects, punishments and reserved sins, when incurred for violating the enclosure.

5. *Matrimonial dispensations:* The Sacred Penitentiaria dispenses or grants faculties to dispense from the publication of banns and from occult impediments, which impede but do not annul marriage, even in view of contracting a marriage of conscience. These faculties do not include the power of dispensing from the impediment of mixed religion or from the proofs of being free to marry again. The Tribunal is not competent in this matter as we shall see later.

The constitution exhorts the Tribunal to abstain from granting dispensations from any impediment in any degree of consanguinity or affinity or spiritual relationship, even though the impediment be a secret one and the cause of scandal if the dispensation is not granted. It should also abstain from permitting such marriages. The reason for this clause is the public nature of the impediments. As to contracted marriages it dispenses from the impediments of secret spiritual relationship and public decency when it is secret.[5] It should abstain from granting dispensations or revalidations in regard to marriages contracted in the first or second degree of consanguinity and affinity, even when the impediments are occult, but the dispensation can be

[5] Benedict XIV, Inst. eccl. 87, n. II. Feije, n. 606, Cf. Chap. IV.

granted when the parties for ten years have been considered lawful man and wife. These two faculties just mentioned may remain after the New Code has the force of law, but since the impediments of affinity and public decency have been changed, the faculties regarding these impediments will have to be remodelled. Affinity arising from illicit intercourse has been entirely abolished and the impediment of public decency has been substantially altered as we shall see later. Affinity according to the New Code canon 97 arises only from lawful wedlock that is, marriage ratum and consummatum or ratum only. We shall omit the faculties contained in the Constitution "Pastor bonus" relating to affinity ex copula illicita and betrothment since these impediments will no longer exist after Pentecost.

The Tribunal can grant a dispensation, when the parties have had intercourse and did not mention the fact in order to obtain the dispensation more easily. Since the decree of Pope Leo XIII issued by the S. C. S. O. on the 25th of June, 1885 and 28th of August, 1895, it is no longer necessary for the validity of the dispensation to mention the fact of having had intercourse. It dispenses from the occult impediment of crime i. e. adultery with the promise of marriage both as to marriages contracted and to be contracted. When in the impediment of crime both parties have participated in homicide, it dispenses only if the crime is entirely secret and then only for reasons that are weighed and approved in the special congress of the Sacred Penitentiaria. All these faculties mentioned extend to the cases, where the impediments are multiple and arise from various sources. The faculties include the power of legitimating children with the exception of those conceived in sacrilege or adultery, which require a special rescript of the Pope. Lastly it answers all questions, solves all doubts and difficulties concerning sins and the penitential forum.

What was stated at the Council of Vienne in the year 1311 and in the Constitution "In elegendis" of Pius IV remains in full force: the faculties of the Sacred Penitentiaria do not expire with the death of the Pope. Benedict XIV says: "We desire and decree that the Major Penitentiary (whose faculties during that time do not expire, but are merely not exercised outside of the conclave), or his officials, can act and expedite all matters concerning the forum of conscience, but absolution is given only ad tempus et cum reincidentia. Those who have been absolved must have recourse to the new Pope within a specified time."

The officials of the Sacred Penitentiaria are not privileged to extend the term.

Pius X in his Constitution "Vacante Sede Apostolica" (Dec. 25th, 1904, n. 12) decreed the following: "The office of the Major Penitentiary does not cease at the death of the Pontiff."[6] "The Major Penitentiary can act and exercise his powers during the vacancy of the Apostolic See as provided for and defined by Benedict XIV in his Constitution "Pastor bonus" (Apr., 1744, par. 51-55). Hence during the vacancy of the Apostolic See the Sacred Penitentiaria enjoys almost unlimited powers regarding the internal forum. Whenever the welfare of souls so demands, it grants absolutions, condonations, dispensations in all matters which cannot be postponed till the election of the new Pope. It can even absolve from penalties and censure regarding which it had no power during the reign of the preceeding Pope.[7]

The absolutions granted under such circumstances however, are valid only for the time being with the obligation to have recourse to Rome when the new Pope has been elected. Regarding the time when recourse must be had, there is no specific law. Benedict XIV says that the time is to be reckoned according to the distance the petitioners are from Rome. We may apply the law here laid down by the S. C. S. O. (June 23, 1886) which demands that in all cases in which the confessor absolves "cum reincidentia" the petition must be made within a month's time.[8]

Benedict XIV in his Constitution grants the Sacred Tribunal the widest faculties regarding dispensations but with these limitations: during the vacancy of the Holy See it can dispense only when the common spiritual welfare of souls is concerned; secondly that the dispensations be diligently examined in the Signatura; thirdly that the consent of the Major Penitentiary, residing at the conclave be obtained and fourthly that recourse be had to the new Pope within a month's time after his election.

For the sake of brevity we have omitted some cases in which the Sacred Penitentiaria can likewise dispense and absolve, but those given will amply suffice to show what it can do in similar circumstances. In consequence of the repeal of the accumulated powers held by the Roman Congregations and Tribunals, each

[6] Clement V cap. Ne Romani pars. 1 de elect. 1, 3 in Clem; Pius IV Const. "In elegendis" par. 9. Clement XII. Const. "Apostolatus Officium" par. 15.

[7] Cappello, De Curia Rom. vol. I p. 115, vol. II p. 85.

[8] Capello l. c. vol. II p. 85.

matter has its appointed place; nevertheless, in particular cases, doubt and error may occur.[9] Under such circumstances it must be remembered that: A favor, denied by one Congregation or Office of the Roman Curia, cannot be validly granted by another Sacred Congregation or Office or local Ordinary with the necessary powers, without the consent of the S. Congregation or Office to which application was first made, the rights of the Sacred Penitentiaria remaining intact (can. 43). If it is necessary to mention the refusal of one Congregation, when applying to another, it is certainly more necessary, when a Congregation and the Ordinary are concerned. If the Ordinary refuses to grant the rescript, the Congregation can validly grant it, even though the fact that the favor was rejected by the Ordinary has not been mentioned. The Sacred Penitentiaria can grant favors and dispensations in the internal forum, when the rescripts have been refused by others because, while the refusal is sometimes necessary for the public welfare, the private good of the individual, with which the Sacred Tribunal is concerned, always prevails.

[9] Normae pecul. cap. I n. 2.

CHAPTER IV

PART I

"Dummodo sit occultum"

In granting dispensations the S. Penitentiaria uses the clause "dummodo sit occultum." We shall endeavor to show in this chapter, what is meant by this term and how far the meaning has been changed by the New Code. To decide, what is public and what is occult, was not an easy task up to the present time. The terms were incumbered by innumberable distinctions, and any author, trying to clarify matters, succeeded only in adding a new opinion to those already in existence.

An impediment was either occult in nature or in fact. Occult by nature meant an impediment, arising from a defamatory act. It was occult in a double sense: materially occult, when the fact from which the impediment had its origin, was unknown; it was formally occult and materially public, when the fact was known, but people were not aware that such a fact constituted an impediment. It was simply occult, when it was known to a few, strictly occult, when only the confessor and the parties bound knew of the impediment.

It was said that an impediment may be public either in nature or in fact, materially public or formally public, strictly public or simply public, materially public and formally occult or both materially public and formally public.[1] Consanguinity, affinity, spiritual relationship, disparity of cult, mixed religion, holy Orders, solemn vows, were considered impediments by nature public even though the fact was not known. The impediment of crime could be public in fact (materially public) and occult as impediment (formally occult), strictly occult, when only the confessor and the parties were aware of it, or simply occult, when it was known to a few other prudent and discrete persons.

Ojetti explained the occult in the following manner: "According to nature and usage of Canon Law, occult is that which is opposed to the manifest (pluribus notum) and the notorious (quod celari non potest). If the fact could be proved by wit-

[1] Gasparri, no. 260; Telch, Epitome p. 320.

nesses, but can still be kept secret, it is considered occult."[2] Bouix speaking of the practice of the S. Penitentiaria holds the same opinion saying: "An impediment can be considered occult even though one or two in a community, three or five in a village, five or eight in a city are aware of the fact."[3] D'Annibale gave the following rule: "It is a question of fact and hence rests with the estimation of the good. It is said to be occult, when so few persons know it, that it can justly be assumed that practically nobody is aware of it."[4]

So far the practice of the S. Penitentiaria has been to dispense from impediments occult by nature, even when the impediment was known to three, four even as many as ten discrete persons, according to the size of the place, and provided there was no danger of publicity.[5] St. Alphonsus says: "I know that the S. Penitentiaria has dispensed in a certain impediment of consanguinity, which was known to about ten persons,"[6] Gasparria adds that the S. Penitentiaria dispensed from an impediment known to seven or eight in a city of 9,000 population.[7]

The difficulty became acute, when it was a question of an impediment materially public but formally occult. Does the S. Penitentiaria include in the clause "*dummodo sit occultum,*" an impediment when the fact from which the impediment has its origin is known, but not that such fact constitutes an impediment? Take the case of a woman, who in agreement with another kills her husband. The crime is public but it is not known that such an act forms a diriment impediment and invalidates the marriage with the accomplice. Benedict XIV says: "We have always considered it a difficult matter and cannot include it in the number of those impediments from which the S. Penitentiaria dispenses under the form "dummodo sit occultum." If this were true," he continues, "then every impediment of crime and affinity, from illicit intercourse, even if they were public, could be classed among the occult. Experience teaches that all impediments, with the exception of consanguinity and affinity arising from licit congress, are unknown, not only to the village people, but also

---

[2] Ojetti, Synop. vol. II p. 2779. Sanchez, VIII disp. 34 n. 55; D'Ann. Com. in Const. Ap. Sed. n. 234; St. Alph. VI 593; Salmant. Theol. Mor. t. XIII c. 4, n. 53.

[3] D. Bouix, Tract. de Cur. R. p. 255; Plettenberg, Notitia Congr. p. 203.

[4] D'Ann. p. 1, par. 242, note 49; Reiff. App. 46.

[5] Gasparri, n. 260; Leitner, p. 410; Putzer, p. 29; Wernz, n. 613, note 36.

[6] Lib. VI no. 1111.

[7] Gasparri, no. 260.

to those living in cities. Finally we can affirm with an oath, that in all those years, when we were associated with the S. Penitentiaria our vote, written or oral, was always concerning an impediment materially public and we never even considered an impediment only formally occult."[8] Giraldi,[9] Santi,[10] Rosset [11] and many others, held the same view with Benedict XIV.

Gasparri maintaines, that the opinion of Benedict XIV was confirmed by a response of the S. Penitentiaria.[12] The question proposed was the following: "Do the faculties granted ordinarily to bishops by the S. Penitentiaria include the power of dispensing from the impediment of affinity in the second degree, arising from illicit intercourse, when the marriage is shortly to be contracte and the impediment is only formally occult but materially public?" The answer was: "Non comprehendi."[13]

Wernz in speaking of this question, does not decide the controversy or remove the difficulty. In the question of the impediment arising from crime he says: "When the crime is only materially public and formally occult, it must be considered public and hence would not be included in the clause "dummodo sit occultum."[14]

"The crime," says Ojetti, "must be formally occult at least in regard to the fact, although it might otherwise be public. If for example a person became irregular on account of homicide and it is believed that death was caused by accident (materially public), or that it was a question of self-defence (formally occult errore facti), the case is still an occult one in view of obtaining a dispensation."[15] "According to some authors," Ojetti continues, "the case can be considered to be occult even when it is known that the man was killed through hatred, but it is not known, that the perpetrator is thereby irregular."[16]

The New Code canon 1037 reads: "An impediment is said to be public, when it can be proved in the external forum, otherwise it is occult." This canon is of the greatest importance and requires some explanation. It is said to be (*censetur*) implies that

---

[8] Inst. Eccl. 87, n. 39 sq. Gasparri, n, 260.

[9] Exp. Iur. Pont. App. II ad lib. IV Decret. n. 3.

[10] App. ad lib. Decret. n. 18.

[11] No. 2738.

[12] Gasparri, no. 260 note 1. S. Penitentiaria Jan. 31, 1876.

[13] Gasparri l. c.

[14] Wernz, no. 214 n. 10; no. 619, note 86; no. 640, note 6.

[15] De Curia Rom. S. Penitentiaria.

[16] Layman, Theol. Mor. I, tit. 5, c. 9, n. 4. D'Ann. 1242, 54.

even though the impediment is in fact occult, when there is a possibility of proof, it must be considered public. When this possibility is wanting, the impediment is occult. All the different distinctions of public and occult impediments are hereby eliminated. Consanguinity for instance, affinity, spiritual relationship etc. when they admit of no proof, are occult by law.

This doctrine is not entirely new. Reiffenstuel said: "An occult impediment is one, which is entirely secret so that it cannot be proved."[17] This is also attested by the practice of the S. Penitentiaria. For the purpose of revalidating marriages, the Tribunal has dispensed from the impediments of the third and fourth degree of consanguinity and of licit affinity in the second degree, if this impediment has remained occult for at least ten years, and from spiritual relationship.[18]

The definition of public and occult impediment in the New Code is the same as that given by Gasparri[19] but with this distinction, that in regard to dispensation, Gasparri interpreted the occult in the sense of most authors, it is occult even when it is known by one or two even ten people, provided there is no danger that it will become public.

This distinction, we believe, can no longer be retained. An impediment henceforth must be considered public or occult in the sense of the New Code. It is said to be public, when it can be proved, and occult when proofs are wanting. The competency of the S. Penitentiaria is restricted to the occult impediments according to canons 258 and 1047. Other congregations, especially the S. C. de S., dispense from the public impediments.

Can the S. Penitentiaria dispense now from the impediment which is materially public but formally occult? The question apparently can be answered in the affirmative. A crime according to the New Code (can. 2197), is materially occult when it is secret as a crime, and formally occult when its imputability is hidden. this distinction is not made in reference to impediments. The impediment is said to be occult, when it cannot be proved in the external forum. We are not allowed to make distinctions, where the law does not distinguish.

---

[17] Reiff. App. n. 44; Sanchez, II, disp. 4, n. 40.

Prosper Fagnanus says: "an occult impediment is one, which can in no way be proved. Comm. cap. 7, n. 45 sq. De Cohabit.

[18] "Pastor bonus" Benedict XIV (Apr. 13, 1744). Inst. Eccl. 87, n. 7 and 11 Gasparri, no. 331.

[19] Gasparri, no. 260.

On January 29, 1881, the S. C. C. decided in favor of this opinion. The New Code in canon 1037 has placed upon it the stamp of approval. The reference in the New Code to can. 1037 corroborates our statement. "Communi iurisprudentia receptum est publicum omnino haberi impedimentum quod, licet actu occultum sit, quandocumque vulgari et probari potest."[20] The clause "dummodo sit occultum" includes therefore an impediment materially public but formally occult. Sanchez had the true answer to the difficulty. The impediment must be considered occult as long as it is not known, that a certain fact constitutes an impediment. In other words the impediment cannot be called public, when it cannot be proved in the external forum, since the quality of publicity according to the sense of law is wanting.[21]

Bonacina held the true opinion, now confirmed by the Code, when he said: "An impediment is said to be occult even when the fact is known, but not that such fact constitutes an impediment, i. e. when the impediment is not public as an impediment."[22] Schnitzer has rightly surmised that with the decision of the S. C. C. just quoted, the case has been closed.[23] Layman, Rodriguez, Reginaldus, St. Alphonsus, D'Annibale, Zitelli, Putzer and others have now the approval of the New Code on this matter. Even Benedict XIV, who held the opposite opinion, was forced to confess, that "fere omnes putare satisfieri Penitentiaria mandato, quo illud iubetur, dummodo sit occultum."[24]

In answer to the question: How can we prove in the external forum, that the impediment is public, we refer to that part of Canon Law, which treats of proofs in the external forum (can. 1747). Evidence or notoriety of fact require no proofs. The testimony of two witnesses on one and the same point, provided that they be above all suspicion and are unshaken in their evidence, is a sufficient proof. A public instrument or other documents, having the force of a public instrument forms adequate testimony. The confession of both parties, or of one only, when corroborated by trustworthy witnesses, constitutes a sufficient proof for the existence of the impediment.

---

[20] S. C. C. Mohilovien seu Tiraspolen 9 Iul. 10 Sep. 1881. Act. S. Sed. vol. 14, p. 155 and 458.

[21] Lib. VIII disp. 24, n. 56.

[22] In tract. de leg. disp. 1 quest. 2, n. 2, 7.

[23] Schnitzer, p. 225.

[24] Inst. 87, par. 42.

The S. Penitentiaria dispenses also from an impediment that was once public, but by the lapse of time, has become occult. Ten years are required to render such an impediment occult.[25] The S. Tribunal does not dispense from an impediment or crime, that has been brought before the court, but when the defendant has been absolved even falsely and unjustly, the crime and the impediment arising from it are considered to be occult.[26]

PART II

As a supplement to the preceding, it will be useful to indicate the important changes regarding impediments, with which the S. Penitentiaria is concerned. Every student of Canon Law and Ecclesiastical History knows that the disciplinary rules of the Church are adapted to the circumstances of the times. Some laws regarding matrimonial impediments enacted in the Lateran Council (1215), were mitigated or entirely obrogated by the Council of Trent. In the Vatican Council some bishops petitioned the Holy See to abolish the diriment impediment of affinity arising from illicit intercourse and to limit the impediment of affinity from licit intercourse to the first degree.[1]

The New Code has made the following changes: "Affinity arises from a valid marriage, be this marriage ratified only, or ratified and consummated. It exists only between the husband and the blood-relatives of the wife, between the wife and the blood-relatives of the husband. It is computed in the following manner: Those who are the blood-relatives of the husband, are in the same degree and line the blood-relatives of the wife and vice versa" (can. 971). Affinity in the direct line invalidates marriage in all degrees, in the collateral line to the second degree inclusive. The impediment becomes multiple; (1) When the impediment of consanguinity from which it arises is multiple; (2) by successive marriages with the blood-relatives of the deceased wife" (can. 1077).

The question of licit or illicit intercourse has no longer any reference to affinity. It arises from marriage only. What formerly partly constituted the impediment of public decency has now been added to affinity. A ratified marriage formerly gave

[25] Twenty to thirty years are required for irregularity. Putzer, p. 30; Benedict XIV. Instr. 87, n. 4 and 7; Gasparri, no. 260.

[26] Sanchez, De Matr. disp. 38, no. 12; Ferraris, Bibliot. under Disp. Putzer, p. 30; Zitelli, disp. p. 51.

[1] Martin, collect docum. Con. Vat. p. 162, 190.

rise to the impediment of public decency, it now gives rise to affinity. The impediment of public decency formerly arose from betrothment or from a ratified marriage. According to the New Code (can. 1078) public decency arises from an invalid marriage, be this marriage consummated or not, and from a public or notorious concubinage. It invalidates marriage in the first and second degree, between the husband and the blood-relatives of the wife and vice versa.

The Church now, as in the past, relaxes the vigor of her laws, when the necessity of the times warrants a change, and tightens the bond in conformity with the spirit of the old Roman Law, which decreed: "In marriage, not only what is lawful, but also what is becoming must always be considered."[2] Illicit intercourse no longer constitutes an impediment of affinity, but public or notorious and repeated congress is now an impediment of public decency.[3]

The fact that the New Code has abolished the impediment of affinity from illicit intercourse demonstrates that it was an impediment, not of the natural law, but of the ecclesiastical law. The Church has followed this doctrine in the past, because through the S. Penitentiaria, she has frequently dispensed from this impediment.[4]

Some authors as Bellarminus, Reiffenstuel, Rosset, Pirhing and others claim that affinity from licit intercourse, has its origin in the natural law, but the majority of canonists rightly maintains, that it is only an ecclesiastical impediment from which the Church can dispense.[5] Examples of dispensations thus granted are found in the Council of Epaon (a. 517, can. 30) and in the Council of Orleans (Conc. Aurel. III a. 538, can. 10), which states that marriage contracted in infidelity with the wife of the father or the daughter of the wife, are not to be considered void after baptism. The S. C. S. O. has decided the question in announcing that "there is no doubt that the Pope has the power to grant dispensation in the first degree of affinity in direct line. Even then,

[2] L. 197, D. L. 17.

[3] Leo XIII in the const. "Trans oceanum (Apr. 18, 1897) limited the impediments of consanguinity and affinity for the Negroes and Indians in Latin America and the Philippines to the second degree. This privilege is not abolished by the New Code.

[4] Gasparri, n. 796; Kernz, n. 430 note 45.

[5] Bellarm. De Matr. lib. II. c. XVIII. note 2; Reiff. Lib. IV tit. XIV no. 49; Rosset, n. 1956; Pirhing, n. 32. Opponents: Sanchez, VII. disp. 66. n. 7; Riganti, Reg. Cancel Ap. no. 20; Gonzalez in cap. I. De cons. et aff, n. 9; De Justis, lib. II c. VII. n. 54; Schmalzgr. lib. IV. t. XIV n. 103; Gasparri, n. 792; Wernz, n. 430 n. 45, etc.

when the impediment arises from licit intercourse, can he allow the step-father to marry his step-daughter."[6]

Granted, however, that the Church has this power, does she ever make use of it? Canonists generally answer in the negative. They base their doctrine, that the Church never dispenses from the impediment arising from licit affinity in the first degree direct line, on the decisions of the Congregations.[7] The S. C. C. (28 May, 1796) emphatically refused to revalidate the marriage of a man with his step-daughter, who was a legitimate child from a former marriage.

In late years the Church has mitigated her laws in this matter. An interesting case is recorded, where the S. Penitentiaria granted a dispensation from the impediment of licit affinity in the first degree in direct line.[8] John T. married S., the mother of Rebecca, who is an illegitimate child. The mother died and John married Rebecca in the year 1907 before the civil magistrate, unaware of the impediment of affinity. It is certain that Rebecca is not the daughter of John. To legitimate their child, to avoid the scandal of a separation and for the welfare of their offspring, they applied for a dispensation. The S. Penitentiaria granted the dispensation in the following form: Sacra Poenitentiaria, mature consideratis peculiaribus adjunctis in casu expositis, de speciali et expressa Apostolica Auctoritate, benigne sic annuente S. S. Dno. Nro Pio Pp. X, Tibi Dilecto in Christo, Oratorum Ordinario facultatem concedit, si ita sit, super recensitis in precibus impedimenentis cum oratoribus benigne dispensandi, ad hoc ut ipsi, omissis proclamationibus sed remoto scandalo, servatis in reliquis canonicis praesumptionibus, matrimonium contrahere in eoque remanere licite ac libere valeant; prolemque sive susceptam sive suscipiendam exinde legitimam declarandi ac respective nuntiandi. Contrariis quibuscumque non obstantibus. Praesentes autem litterae custodiantur, ut pro quocumque futuro eventu de matrimonii validitate et prolis legitimate constare possit. Datum Romae, in Sacra Poenitentiaria, die 2 Dec. 1911.

This is an extraordinary dispensation and was granted only by special permission of the Pope. It is interesting in more than one way. When it was proposed to the S. C. de Sacr., the Congregation refused to grant the dispensation. Although the im-

---

[6] S. C. S. O. Feb. 14, 1727; Sep. 4, 1743; Feb. 20, 1888; Aug. 26, 1891.

[7] S. C. C. Liège May 28, 1796; S. C. S. O. Feb. 20, 1888; Aug. 26, 1891, in collect, S. C. de P. F. n. 1471, 1247. Wernz, n. 438 note 70; Gasparri, n. 796.

[8] Vermeersch in Nouv. Rev. Theol. Sep. p. 528; Le Can. Contemp. vol. 35, p. 658.

pediment is formally and by nature public, it was was brought before the S. Penitentiaria which, since the reform of the Curia, dispenses only from occult impediments and was, by special command of the Pope decided by the same. The doctrine therefore repeated by canonists in general, that the Church, though she possesses the power to dispense in the impediment of affinity in the first degree direct line, does not do so, admits of some exceptions. Our case is an exceptional one, but we must bear in mind, that it is nevertheless an actual occurrence, the knowledge of which might be useful in similar instances. On the other hand we must guard against drawing rash conclusions. Vermeersch concludes from this decision, that it is no longer impossible to obtain in exceptional cases a dispensation, that the step-father may marry the legitimate daughter of his deceased wife. There is no essential differnce in the impediment of affinity, he states, whether the daughter be lgitimate or illegitimate. A. Bouhinhon, in Le Canoniste Contemporain, believes that the conclusion goes too far. Even though, he says, there is no difference in the causes of the impediment, the juridical effects are not the same. Licit and illicit affinity also had the same causes, but the effects in law were quite different. Illicit affinity invalidated marriage only to the second degree; occult illicit affinity was removed by a dispensation in the forum of conscience; finally it does not exist at all in the civil law and was abolished by the New Code. Hence it cannot be denied that the nature of the origin makes a great difference not only in regard to law, according to which a legitimate child enjoys privileges entirely different from those of an illegitimate, but also in regard to obtaining a dispensation. We can easily understand, therefore, why the Church would grant the dispensation in the one case and would refuse to do so in the other. Another dispensation analogous to the one mentioned by Vermeersch, was granted by Pope Leo XIII (1894).[9] The Church beyond a doubt has the power to dispense from the impediment of affinity in direct line and can permit a man to marry his step-daughter or step-mother, or a woman to marry her step-son or step-father even when it is a question of a legitimate offspring. But if the Church does dispense, she does so rarely and only for very grave reasons. The Church is a kind mother and relaxes her laws, when the public welfare is not placed in jeopardy, and not even in the most desperate cases should all hope be abandoned.[10]

---

[9] J. B. Ferreris, Los. Esp. y. el Matr. 1916. no. 628 sq.
[10] Sabetti-Barrett, no. 892.

CHAPTER V

The Giver of Matrimonial Dispensations and Causes for Which Dispensations May be Granted

So far we have studied the history, constitution and competency of the Sacred Tribunal. To make this study practical, we shall endeavor to point out ways and means to be employed by those, who will be called upon to apply for dispensations.

Matrimonial dispensations have for their author the Pope, the Roman Congregation, the Bishop or Ordinary and the priest.

Preliminary observations: According to the legislation of "Sapienti consilio" the impediments have been divided into minor and major impediments.[1] This change is of the greatest importance, since "dispensations for the minor impediments shall be granted for reasonable causes approved by the Holy See; under this form they will have the same force as if given in virtue of a Motu proprio and with certain knowledge and so will not be open to question on the ground either of obreption or subreption."[2] The New Code makes this even stronger. In Canon 1054 we read: "A dispensation granted for a minor impediment is not vitiated either by obreption or subreption even though the final cause given in the petition be false." Hence even when the determining or final cause is false the dispensation for a minor impediment is valid. The Pope, the Congregation or the Ordinary act of their own accord and with a presumed knowledge of the case as though no dispensation had been asked and hence omission of some truth or an assertion of something false, does not vitiate the dispensation. In the New Code this division of minor and major impediments has been substantially retained but some of the minor impediments have been entirely abolished as the third degree of affinity and the fourth degree of consanguinity, public decency arising from betrothment or marriage ratified. The impediment of crime formerly among the major is now classed among the minor impediments. The minor impediments according to can. 1042 are the following:

1. Consanguinity in the third degree collateral line.
2. Affinity in the second degree collateral line.

---

[1] Normae pecul. cap. VII art. 3.

[2] Normae pecul. no. 21 art. 3.

3. Public decency in the second degree.
4. Spiritual relationship.
5. The impediment of crime arising from adultery with the promise of marriage or an attempted civil marriage.

All other impediments are major impediments.

This important change was primarily made for the S. Cong. of the Sacraments. The question then arose: Can this law be extended to the Sacred Penitentiaria and the Ordinary? It was quite generally admitted that the competency of the Sacred Penitentiaria enjoyed the same privileges in the internal forum as the Sacred Cong. of the Sacraments in the external forum.[3] The other question, whether Bishops or Ordinaries can grant dispensations "*ex motu proprio*," gave rise to different opinions. Sanchez stated: "It would seem to be more proper that the Ordinary grant dispensations motu proprio, because he is better acquainted with the circumstances of the case than even the Pope."[4] Schmalzgrueber,[5] Reiffenstuel,[6] De Smet[7] and others held the same opinion.

The opinion of these authors has received the sanction of the New Code. Rescripts according to can. 36 are not only granted by the Apostolic See but by Ordinaries as well. The division of impediments into minor and major is a general one and enjoys the force of law not only in the S. C. of the Sacraments but for all who can exercise voluntary jurisdiction. It is self-evident that, when a dispensation from a minor impediment has been granted, it does not mean that the parties are free to marry, when other impediments not mentioned are present. A reasonable cause for dispensation is necessary in all cases, because it cannot be supposed that dispensation is granted at random, but practically it is invariably present when the petition is made.

A just and proportionate cause is always demanded if not for the validity, at least for the licitness of a dispensation, when there is question of a major impediment.[8] The New Code can. 84 enacted the following: "No one should dispense from an ec-

---

[3] De Smet, no. 375 note 3; Genicot-Salmant. II p. 715; Capello, p. 375.

[4] Sanchez, lib. VIII disp. 21 no. 48.

[5] Schmalzgrueber, vol. V. p. 111 tit. XVI no. 147.

[6] Reiffenstuel, App. par. 9 no. 420.

[7] De Smet, no. 375 note 3.

[8] Conc. Trid. Sess. XXIV cap. 5 de ref. matr; Sess. XXV cap. 18; Instr. S. C. de P. F. May 9, 1877; Suarez, De Leg. lib. VI cap. 18; Conc. Balt. II no 335 Collect. Lace. t. III collect. 488.

clesiastical law without a just and reasonable cause, which cause must be in proportion to the gravity of the law from which dispensation is granted. If an inferior dispenses without such a cause, the dispensation is illicit and invalid."

To dispense from a major impediment licitly, and for an inferior to do so validly, the following conditions are necessary: (1) a true and proportionate cause; (2) existing at the time, when the dispensation is granted. To decide whether a cause is sufficient, it is necessary to consider the status of the petitioner and the nature of the impediment. Formerly, when the parties had contracted marriage in bad faith, they lost all rights to leniency.[9] Today the Church is more lenient and grants dispensations not only when one of the parties but even when both parties are in bad faith, provided there is a sufficient cause. She only demands for licitness, that this circumstance be mentioned in the petition. She mitigates her severity to render the legitimation of the children possible.[10] A graver cause is required for some than for others. Not even the Pope can dispense validly without a just cause from vows, from solemn profession, from the marriage ratified of the faithful or in regard to the Pauline privilege, because it is a question of divine law.[11] It is of the greatest importance to follow the custom of the Roman Curia and consider the causes in the light of equity, decency and expediency. Modern authors are continually insisting on this practice and persistently advise that the Ordinary for validity follow the style of the Curia when dispensing in virtue of delegated powers, and for the sake of uniformity when the dispensation is granted by ordinary powers.[12] The reason is plain. When the Pope by privilege or special faculties grants any one the power to dispense from certain impediments, he wishes the delegate to conform to his wishes and use the faculties in the same way and for the same causes.[13]

The causes for which dispensations are granted, are either canonical or non-canonical. Canonical causes are those expressly admitted by the Holy See. As many as twenty-eight have been enumerated, but most authors reduce the number to sixteen or

---

[9] Conc. Trid. Sess. XXIV cap. 5 de ref.

[10] Gasparri, no. 348.

[11] Noldin, I n. 164, 171; Laymann, Theol. mor. T I tr. 4. c. 22. n. 15; Telch, p. 357.

[12] Wernz, no. 620, note 95.

[13] Reiffenstuel lib. III tit. 35. no. 77; Putzer, no. 11, 12.

eighteen.[14] We refer to these different authors for explanation of the various causes.

The Instruction of the S. C. de P. F. (May 9, 1879) after enumerating the different causes states: "These are the more common and the chief causes which can be alleged for matrimonial dispensations." These words indicate, that other non-canonical causes can be adduced and approved. The Sacred Penitentiaria and the Dataria in the past have repeatedly granted dispensations for non-canonical causes. Thus a strong desire on the part of the parents in favor of the marriage, when a particular benefit could be derived from the union, when the parties ignorant of any impediment before marriage, became aware of it immediately afterwards, were sufficient causes. The S. C. S. O. (Aug. 14, 1822) answered in the affirmative, when asked by the Apost. Vicar of Bosnia, whether "vesanus amor (a strong affection) combined with the danger of contracting civil marriage" would be a sufficient cause for a dispensation.[15]

It is the practice of the Holy See to be more lenient in granting dispensations when the petitioner is the offspring of an illegitimate union, or to one who is physically deformed. It grants dispensations more easily to widowers or widows with children. A strong purpose of marriage, the good of both parties or the parents, public good and the like, under certain circumstances constitute sufficient causes.[16] When graver causes are wanting, several minor causes, though insufficient in themselves have been admitted by the Holy See, on account of their number.[17]

Rome has frequently granted dispensatione for "certain reasonable causes," especially to princes and those in high positions. Dispensations thus granted were sometimes called "dispensationes sine causa," not because no causes were present, but because none were mentioned to avoid danger of defamation.[18] When there are sufficient honorable causes, dishonorable or defamatory causes should not be mentioned, especially, when the defamatory causes are occult.

The second condition for the dispensation in major impediments is: The cause must be present at the time, when the dispensation is granted. Dispensations are granted either in forma

[14] Gasparri, vol. I, p. 239, ed. III; Wernz, no. 519, vol. IV, ed. II; Noldin, vol. III, no. 630; De Smet, no. 374.

[15] Gasparri, no. 366.

[16] Leitner, p. 431; Wernz, no. 631.

[17] Reiff. App. no. 120; Sanchez, lib. VIII disp. 19, no. 34.

[18] Reiff. App. no. 98; Schmalzgr. pars III. tit. XVI no. 135.

gratiosa or in forma commissoria. When the dispensation is granted in forma gratiosa, the cause must be true when the dispensation is given; if granted in forma commissoria, it must be true when the dispensation is executed (can. 38). The opinions formerly differed in this matter.[19]

To omit some truth (subreptio) in the petition, does not render the rescript void or invalid, provided everything is expressed, which, according to the Style of the Curia, is demanded for validity. Neither does a false assertion (obreptio) vitiate the rescript, provided the one motive cause alleged, or at least one from among the many causes proposed, be true. Obreption or subreption in one part of the rescript does not invalidate any other part of the rescript that contains more than one favor (can. 42).

A dispensation may be licitly applied for and licitly granted when there is doubt about the sufficiency of the cause (can. 84). A probably just cause suffices not only for licitly asking a dispensation, but even for granting it licitly. If in doubt whether the dispensation was granted for a just cause, the dispensation is valid even though the cause appears less just after it has been awarded. This rule can be applied when in doubt, whether the dispensation has been asked for or whether it was reasonably and validly granted.[20] The application of this rule can be extended to the powers enjoyed by delegate and executor.[21]

Summing up, then, we distinguish between minor and major impediments. A reasonable cause suffices for a dispensation from the minor impediments. Omitting some truth or asserting something false does not vitiate the dispensation.

A true, just and proportionate cause is necessary for the dispensation from the major impediments; and, provided such cause is mentioned and present, when the dispensation is granted, the omission of some truth, ignorance, bad faith or even falsehood, though sinful, does not render the dispensation void. The penalty for the abuse of dispensations is mentioned in canon 2361. Any one, who through fraud or trickery has omitted the truth or asserted something false in the supplica sent to the Apostolic See or the Ordinary, should be punished by his Ordinary according to the gravity of the offense.

---

[19] Reiff. App. n. 221; Schmalzgr. lib. IV. t. 16. n. 161.

[20] D'Annibale, I. n. 233.

[21] De Justis, disp. matr. 3. c. I. n. 84; St. Alph. Theol. Mor. I. 6. n. 902; Sanchez, lib. VIII. disp. 21. n. 25.

CHAPTER VI

Dispensations and Absolutions Granted by Ordinaries in Virtue of Ordinary Powers

When the nature of the impediment is known and a sufficient cause for the dispensation has been found, the next step in the procedure will be to inquire: to whom shall one apply for the dispensation?

Experience teaches that, notwithstanding the fact that asking and granting dispensations are of daily occurence, doubts and difficulties are encountered at every turn, because the style and practice are not well understood and followed. Dispensations are asked which can never be granted, and petitioners are dissuaded from applying when the matter could easily be adjusted. Many have recourse to Rome, when the Ordinary could grant the necessary powers, or they apply to the S. Penitentiaria in matters, where the S. C. de Sacr. or one of the other congregations are alone competent. We shall give a brief survey of the theory and practice of dispensations in conformity with the New Code.

When jurisdiction, either ordinary or delegated, is granted for the external forum, it is also valid for the internal forum, but not vice versa. But jurisdiction granted for the internal forum may also be exercised in the internal extra-sacramental forum, unless the sacramental forum is indicated. If the forum for which jurisdiction has been given is not mentioned, the faculties are considered to be granted for both, unless the forum is defined by the nature of the case (can. 202).

When several impediments present themselves, some from which the Bishop can dispense, the others reserved to the Pope, the Bishop's power is suspended and papal dispensation must be obtained first. If however, after papal dispensation has been procured, other impediments are discovered from which the Bishop can dispense, the Bishop may exercise his faculties (can. 1050). When application has been made to the Holy See in a matter of an impediment from which the Bishop can dispense by delegated faculties, the Bishop should not use his powers, except in cases of urgent necessity (can. 1048). In an urgent case however he can make use of his faculties but he must notify the Holy See immediately (can. 204).

We must bear in mind that there are impediments of the natural law and impediments of the ecclesiastical law. Prohibitive impediments of the natural law are those arising from vows. Diriment impediments of the natural law are: error, violence and fear, ligamen, impotency, consanguinity certainly in the first degree direct line, beyond that probably, in the collateral line in the first degree also probably.[1]

The power of the Sovereign Pontiff in dispensing from matrimonial impediments extends to all impediments of the ecclesiastical law. This is implied by canon 1040 which reads: None but the Roman Pontiff can abrogate prohibitive or diriment impediments of the ecclesiastical law, nor can any one derogate or dispense from them unless he has received such power from common law or by special indult of the Apostolic See.

The reason is apparent. The lawgiver who enacts laws and sanctions customs can naturally abrogate them or dispense from them for sufficient reasons. He could dispense from them, validly even without reason, though not licitly.[2] Vows are of the divine law but only conditionally, since the obligations arising from them are dependent on the free will of man. The Pope in virtue of the powers granted to him by God can free his subjects from these obligations for grave reasons. Not even the Pope can dispense from the divine-natural law, when this law, as for instance, impotency, is absolute and independent of the acts of man.[3]

In some ecclesiastical impediments the Pope never dispenses, in others he dispenses rarely. He never dispenses from the impediment of crime, when the murder is public, nor from the Order of Episcopacy. He seldom dispenses from the impediments of affinity in the direct line, Order of the Priesthood or solemn profession. Ordinarily the Pope does not dispense from an impediment doubtful as to the law or as to the fact in the absolute natural law.[4]

ORDINARY POWERS OF THE SACRED CONGREGATIONS

According to the constitution "Sapienti consilio" and the New Code the following congregations have each their powers to grant dispensations from matrimonial impediments: The S. Penitentiaria for the internal forum in ecclesiastical impediments, occult

[1] Wernz, no. 612; Reiff. App. n. 6; Schmalzgr. p. III, tit. XIV. n. 65.

[2] Schmalzgrueber, p. III, tit. XVI, no. 59.

[3] Wernz, no. 612; Reiff. App. no. 6. Schmalzgr. p. III. tit. XVI, no. 65; Sanchez, lib. VIII. disp. VI. no. 2. Santi, lib. III, tit. XXXIV. 13 sq.

[4] S. C. S. O. April 6, 1906; De Smet, no. 350; Wernz, no. 612.

in the sense pointed out; for the external forum, the S. C. de P. F., the S. C. S. O.; the S. C. for the Affairs of the Religious Orders, especially the S. C. of the Discipline of the Sacraments. By a Motu proprio of Benedict XV (May 1, 1917) the S. C. for the Oriental Church enjoys all faculties, which other Congregations have for the churches of the Latin Rite, the jurisdiction of the S. C. S. O. remaining intact.[5] For the various powers we refer to what has been said.[6]

ORDINARY POWERS OF THE BISHOP

Only when the secrecy of the confessional is in danger, the priest or confessor will be called upon to have recourse directly to the Holy See. The easiest and the proper way will be, to apply in all other cases to the Bishop, who can dispense and absolve either by ordinary or delegated powers in most cases. Unless the Bishop has special faculties he cannot grant general absolutions or dispensations from irregularity, matrimonial impediments, solemn vows, reserved vows, or from any other cases not reserved by himself personally.

(a) In virtue of ordinary faculties the Ordinary can dispense from *oaths* unless there is question of justice to a third party, in which case the Holy See, for grave reasons can alone dispense (can. 1320).

(b) Ordinaries can dispense their subjects, either themselves or through a delegate, from all *irregularities*, arising from an occult crime. They cannot dispense voluntary homicides, abortionists (effectu secuto) and their cooperators, and those whose cases are before court (can. 990).

(c) Ordinaries can dispense their subjects and strangers within their territory from *vows* not reserved to the Pope, provided there is a just cause and no violation of the rights of others (can. 1313). Ordinaries can dispense from the *reserved vows*, viz. perpetual and perfect vow of chastity and the vow of joining an Order with solemn vows, when they were made conditionally and before the completion of the eighteenth year (can. 1309). They can dispense from these two vows in case of doubt or urgent necessity.[7]

(d) Absolution from censure and dispensation from vindictive punishments, can be granted by him, who has inflicted the

---

[5] Act. Ap. Sed. vol. no. II, p. 529.

[6] Wernz, no. 613; De Smet, no. 351.

[7] Reiff. App. n. 13; Schmalzgr. III. it. XVI. n. 117; De Smet, n. 357; Canon 81.

penalty, by his superior, successor or one, who has been entrusted with such powers (can. 2236). In occult cases the Ordinary can absolve, in person or through a delegate, from all penalties latae sententiae of the common law, except from those which are particularily or in a special manner reserved to the Holy See (can. 2237). The Ordinary enjoys additional powers in cases of urgent necessity, which are indicated under faculties of confessor.

PROHIBITIVE IMPEDIMENTS

The Bishop, by an express (Conc. Trid. sess XXIV c. 1 de ref.) or tacit (X c. 2 de eo qui IV 13) concession of law, can dispense from all prohibitive impediments excepting those reserved to the Holy See or some one superior to the Bishop.[8] The Ordinary can now permit the solemn celebration of matrimony during the forbidden times (can. 1108). When the parents refuse their consent to a marriage the case must be referred to the Ordinary (can. 1034). Unless the Ordinary enjoys delegated powers, he cannot dispense from vows reserved to the Pope, mixed religion, the prohibition of the Pope, Metropolitan or any other superior in case of appeal.[9] Exceptions to this rule are made in canon 81 of which we have spoken above.

DIRIMENT IMPEDIMENTS

In virtue of his ordinary faculties the Ordinary can dispense in the general law of the Church, when recourse to the Holy See is difficult and the case is urgent and of such a nature that the Holy See would dispense (can. 81). Ordinaries can do nothing in regard to the universal law, not even in particular cases, unless the three following conditions conjointly are present: (1) difficulty of recourse to Rome; (2) grave danger in delay; (3) the case is one in which the Church is accustomed to dispense.

1. The difficulty may be either *moral* as for instance, danger of defamation or incontinency, or *physical*. About three weeks may be considered as necessary for obtaining a dispensation from the Holy See.[10] Since the difficulty to have recourse to Rome can easily be obviated by writing a letter, poverty, inexperience in traveling or the like excuses, have lost their importance and can no longer be alleged as excuses.[11] It is not necessary to apply for

[8] Wernz, no. 615; De Smet, no. 357; Gasparri, no. 434; Sanchez, disp. 40, n. 14.

[9] Wernz, no. 615; Sanchez, VIII disp. 5, no. 1.

[10] Archiv. f. k. Kirchenrecht, 1902, p. 493; De Smet, no. 355.

[11] S. C. Inq. June 23, 1886; Wernz, 618.

a dispensation by telegraph, because the Holy See regularily does not admit petitions sent by such means.[12]

2. *Danger in delay:* Which would be the case if, on the one hand, the parties could not be seperated without scandal or disgrace, and if, on the other hand, there is danger of incontinency.

3. *From which the Pope is aecustomed to dispense:* If the Pope cannot dispense or does not wish to dispense, the Ordinary must abstain from granting the dispensation.

The Bishop could formerly dispense, when these conditions were present, in virtue of a tacit [13] consent of the Pope and in character of ordinary powers. Ordinaries can do so now by force of law. Formerly the Bishop's power extended only to the internal forum, to a consummated marriage, contracted with the formalities prescribed by the Church, and when at least one of the parties was in good faith. Canon 81 eliminates these conditions and includes marriages to be contracted. It makes no difference, whether the impediment is occult or public or even multiple. The law is general and does not exclude the faculty of cumnulating.

Formerly good faith was demanded in at least one of the parties. The Council of Trent (sess XIV cap. 5 de ref.) says: "If any one shall knowingly presume to contract marriage within the forbidden degrees, he shall be separated without hope of obtaining dispensation." Most authors demanded good faith in at least one of the parties,[14] but, by reason of the more indulgent attitude of the Church, this power seems to include the revalidation of marriage contracted in bad faith.

DISPENSATIONS WHEN THERE IS IMMINENT DANGER OF DEATH

"When there is imminent danger of death, the Ordinaries, for the quieting of conscience and if necessary for the legitimation of children, can dispense their subjects everywhere and all those living within their territory, from the formalities required for the celebration of matrimony and from all impediments, public, occult or multiple, of the ecclesiastical law, with the exception of the impediments arising from the Order of the Priesthood or affinity in direct line, provided the marriage has been consummated, there be no scandal, and if dispensation is granted from

---

[12] Secret. Status Dec. 10, 1891; Wernz, no. 618, note 80.

[13] Wernz, no. 617, note 72.

[14] Sanchez, II disp. 40, no. 4; Reiff, App. 57 sq.; Schmalzgr. p. 111, tit. XVI no. 81; Wernz, no. 618; Gasparri, no. 440.

disparity of cult or mixed religion, the required conditions have been observed" (can. 1043).

1. "*Urgente mortis periculo*": Persons in respect of whom the Ordinaries have power to dispense are not only the dying concubinarii as formerly, but all subjects wherever they may reside and all strangers actually living within the territory. According to the declaration of the S. C. S. O. (July 1, 1891) they can dispense in favor of a dying person, even when the impediment directly affects the party in good health and not the sick person. As the faculties of Pius X, these ordinary powers apply even to those not sick but who are in imminent danger of death, provided that they wish to set their conscience right or to legitimate their children.[15] The canon says "*urgente mortis periculo*" not "*articulo*," hence one is at liberty to act, when there is grave danger of death.[16] Such danger may arise from any source such as war etc.

2. "*Ad consulendum conscientiae*". This would obtain, for instance, if the man wished to repair the wrong done to the woman or to put on end to scandal or in order to remove the cause of temptation by marriage.

3. "*Si casus ferat legitimationi prolis.*" Either this one or the preceding cause would be sufficient to grant the dispensation.

4. "*Tum super formae, etc.*" In virtue of this power the Ordinaries can dispense from all formalities which are required for the celebration of matrimony. The Ordinaries of China petitioned the Holy See to grant them the faculty to dispense from the presence of the parish priest and two witnesses on account of the peculiar conditions existing in some places of China. The S. C. C. (July 28, 1908) granted the necessary powers.[17] In virtue of this canon these faculties in the character of ordinary powers are now enjoyed by every Ordinary of the place.

5. "*Tum super omnibus et singulis impedimentis, etc.*" This power extends to all impediments, prohibitive and diriment, not merely to the diriment as formerly in virtue of the decree of the S. C. C. (Feb. 20, 1888). The impediments may be either public or occult or even multiple, hence the power includes the faculty of cumulating, as was the case formerly according to some authors.[18] Unless however the Ordinary has delegated

---

[15] "Ne temere" Art. VII.

[16] S. C. de Sacr. Aug. 16, 1909.

[17] Acta S. Sed. XLI 1908, 511.

[18] Wernz, no. 617, note 67.

faculties he cannot grant a "*sanatio in radice*," since such revalidation can be granted only by the Apostolic See (can. 1141).[19]

6. "*Exceptis impedimentis, etc.*" The impediments arising from the Order of the Priesthood and affinity in direct line are not included in these powers. As no distinction is made, affinity is understood in every degree.. Apart from these impediments, the Ordinaries can dispense from all impediments of ecclesiastical law, including the impediment of crime arising from public murder of the partner, the impediment of solemn vows and of Orders below the Priesthood.

It mentions "form of matrimony" separately because the New Code does not class defect of form among the impediments proper. Defect of consent, as error, violence and fear or defect of form, render the marriage invalid but are not properly called diriment impediments.[20]

7. "*Remoto scandalo.*" The means of removing the scandal are left to the good judgment of the Ordinary. A declaration made by the parties before the priest and witnesses, that they are sorry and ask pardon suffices, if the separation of the parties "*a toro et mensa*" cannot be effected conveniently. Some authors required the observance of this clause for the validity and others for licitness.[21] Since the reform of the Curia the tendency of the Holy See has been to make the formalities easier. In virtue of can. 39 this condition is not demanded for the validity of the dispensation. Only those conditions must be observed for validity of the rescript, which are expressed by "*si*," "*dummodo*" or equivalent terms; others are required for licitness only.

8. "*Praestitis consuetis cautionibus.*" The Church according to canon 1061 does not dispense from the impediments of mixed religion or disparity of cult unless: (1) there be a just and grave cause, (2) the non-Catholic party promises to remove danger of perversion from the Catholic party and both promise the Catholic baptism and education of all children, (3) there be moral certainty that these conditions will be fulfilled. These conditions should as a rule be given in writing. The decree of the S. C. S. O. (June 21, 1912) expressly states, that a dispensation is null, when it has been "granted in the matter of the impediment of disparity of worship, by one having faculties from the Holy See, without the exaction, or with the refusal of the precaution-

[19] Leitner, p. 491; Cf. Formularium S. C. S. O. p. 58; Wernz, n. 617, note 67.

[20] Wernz, no. 216.

[21] De Smet, no. 391, p. 316, vol. II.

ary conditions."[22] Notwithstanding these precautions, we believe that canon 39 just mentioned can be applied here. If the Ordinary for no reason dispenses without exacting the conditions, the dispensation would be valid but illicit.

9. *"Consummato matrimonio."* We believe that canon 39 applies here also. The condition is required for licitness only, not for the validity of the dispensation. When the marriage is not consummated, the Ordinary should investigate, whether the conditions mentioned in canon 81 are present and make use of his ordinary faculties mentioned there, or in a so-called perplexed case, apply the faculties granted him for such circumstances.

The Ordinarii locorum dispense from these same impediments and with the same reservations as to scandal, mixed religion and disparity of worship, in a so-called *perplexed case.* A perplexed case is one, in which an impediment is detected, when all preparations for marriage have been made and the marriage cannot be postponed without probably grave evil to the parties, before recourse can be had to the Apostolic See (canon 1044). This faculty was formerly accorded to Ordinaries by tacit consent of the Holy See and only in regard to occult diriment impediments.[23] It was stated, that if not even the Major Penitentiary enjoys the power to dispense from public impediments, it would certainly not be permitted to Ordinaries.[24] Ordinaries now enjoy these powers in favor of all their subjects and all those who reside within their territory. Public impediments are included in this faculty and dispensations can be granted even when one or both parties are in bad faith.

"Sine probabili gravis mali periculo." Reasonable belief that there is danger of evil consequences suffices. Evil which may affect either the body, soul or fortune. To avoid the evils of a civil marriage, would be sufficient cause to grant the dispensation. The evil consequences need not be certain, probable danger of defamation or grave inconvenience, if the impediment were made known, suffices to grant the dispensation.

Canon 1045, 2. Not only do Ordinaries enjoy these powers in regard to perplex cases, for marriages to be contracted, but even for the revalidation of contracted marriages, provided there is danger in delay of having recourse to the Holy See. Authors defended the opinion, that an ecclesiastical impediment discovered by one of the parties after the marriage had been contracted in

[22] Acta Ap. Sed. IV, p. 443.
[23] Wernz, no. 618.
[24] Rosset, no. 2396; Wernz, no. 619, note 85.

good faith and with all the formalities, ceases, if the other party cannot be notified, or revalidation in radice speedily obtained and the marriage debt cannot be easily refused.[25] Other authors refused to admit that impediments cease in a perplexed case, but on account of the extrinsic authority of so many, especially St. Alphonsus, permitted the use of it in practice, hoping that the Holy See would decide the controversy. The Code favors the opinion, which maintains that the impediments do not cease in a perplexed case, but grants the most liberal faculties to dispense under such circumstances.[26] With the restrictions as to scandal and the two impediments mentioned, the Ordinary can dispense in all cases provided there is a physical or moral danger in delay of having recourse to Rome. The impediments arising from Holy Orders of the Priesthood and affinity are the only exceptions.

Ordinarily the priest, not the Bishop, will have to deal with the perplexed case first, we will therefore give a more detailed account of the case, when treating of the powers granted to priests. (N. B. *Forma matr.* is excluded here but see, can. 81.)

POWERS OF ORDINARIES IN REGARD TO DOUBTFUL IMPEDIMENTS

According to the New Code impediments have their origin from certain facts and no reference is had to the person's intention. No ignorance of the law which renders a person incapable or invalidates an act excuses unless the law makes special provisions (can. 16). Ignorance excuses no one from incurring a diriment impediment, or an irregularity "*ex defectu.*" An irregularity "*ex delicto*" can only be contracted, when the act committed is a mortal sin (can. 986).

Ecclesiastical impediments or irregularities that are doubtful from a doubt of law, require no dispensation. The rule is "*lex dubia non obligat*"; a doubtful impediment is no impediment.[27] Laws, even those that render a person inhabilis or invalidate the act, when doubtful from a doubt of law are not binding(can. 15). This opinion was formerly commonly accepted, but it now enjoys the sanction of the Code. Hence matrimony is licit and valid even though the Holy See declares afterwards, that the impediment is certain. The marriage would be valid in the case where the greater probability militates for the existence of the impedi-

[25] Lehmkuhl, Theol. mor. t. II ed. II 1910, n. 1054; Ballerini Palmieri, VI no. 307; Gennari, Consult. moral. can. 2, p. 716; Noldin, III no. 656.

[26] Feije, no. 645; Rosset, no. 2400 sq. Wernz, no. 619.

[27] Sanchez, VIII disp. 6, n. 18; Schmalzgr. IV tit. XVI, n. 76; Gasparri, n. 262.

ment. The priest is of course admonished to apply to the Ordinary for instruction if time permits. The Ordinary in that case does not dispense but simply declares that no impediment exists, or if he does dispense, he dispenses only "ad cautelam." When the Ordinary thinks that the doubt is not well founded, he refers the matter to Rome for an authentic solution.

An impediment that is doubtful from a doubt of fact, cannot be presumed to be non-existent hence requires a dispensation. According to the best authors the Bishop formerly enjoyed ordinary powers to dispense in the internal forum from occult doubtful impediments.[28] This opinion was confirmed by a response of the S. C. C. (Sep. 8, 1852) and the S. C. Inq. (Aug. 3, 1873).[29] Canon 15 has removed all vestige of doubt. The Ordinaries can dispense from laws which are doubtful from a doubt of fact, providing the laws are such in which the Roman Pontiff is accustomed to dispense. In practice the following rules should be observed. If the Ordinary is morally certain that there is no impediment, he permits the celebration of marriage without dispensation and, should there be an impediment, it would cease according to most authors.[30] Imprudent doubts, rumors or one witness, who announces the impediment in a letter, or even when the witness makes a deposition and confirms it with an oath but is not trustworthy, are not sufficient to prove the existence of an impediment, unless the circumstances render the matter really probable.[31] If it is probable that an impediment exists, the Ordinary grants a dispensation, at least ad cautelam. In a contracted marriage, the Ordinary should never proceed to dissolve the union, unless he is obsolutely certain that no dispensation is possible and the impediment is attested by the sworn testimony of trustworthy persons.[32] When the impediment is certain he procures a dispensation or a sanatio in radice as the case may be.[33] The Church rarely dispenses the faithful from doubtful impediments of the natural law. She permits marriage for instance, when impotency is doubtful, "because it is dangerous to refuse a man the right to marriage, when the matter is doubtful."[34] The

---

[28] Wernz, n. 619, note 92; St. Alph. I, n. 194, VI n. 902; Feije, n. 636; Gasparri, n. 438; Sanchez, II disp. XL; D'Ann. p. 111, par. 498, n. 26.

[29] Gasparri, n. 438.

[30] Gasparri, n. 265; Sanchez, VIII disp. 6, n. 18; St. Alph. lib. VI n. 902.

[31] Gasparri, l. c.

[32] Gasparri, n. 266.

[33] Sanchez, L. VIII disp. 6, n. 18; Gasparri, n. 267.

[34] D'Annibale, p. 111, n. 447, note 42; Gasparri, n. 269.

S. C. S. O. often has permitted marriage in such cases. Man has a perfect right to matrimony, and, unless the existence of an impediment before and especially after marriage is certain, the natural right of man prevails.

Canon 15 does not restrict the powers of Ordinaries to occult doubtful impediments, hence the opinion of many authors, that the ordinary powers extend to doubtful public impediments, is now certain.[35]

RULES REGULATING THESE POWERS

Ordinaries: By a decree of the S. C. Inq. (Feb. 20, 1888) Leo XIII determined, what is meant by Ordinary. The New Code has not substantially changed anything in this matter. "Unless expressly excluded, besides the Roman Pontiff, Ordinaries by law are: the residential Bishop for his territory, Abbot and Praelatus nullius, their Vicars General, Administrators, Vicar and Prefect Apostolic, all those who by law or approved constitutions succeed them in office, and for their subjects, the major superior of exempted clerical Orders. (2) Ordinaries of a place or places are all those mentioned with the exception of religious superiors" (can. 198).

When it is difficult to have recourse to Rome, but the difficulty can be obviated by applying to one who has special faculties, for example the papal delegate, the Ordinaries must apply to the delegate.[36]

Formerly, when a dispensation had been granted from an occult impdiment and the impediment became public afterwards, another dispensation for the external forum was necessary.[37] Gasparri claimed that a new dispensation is only required ad cautelam, which opinion was confirmed by a response of the S. C. C. (Jan. 28, 1881).[38] Canon 1047 referring to rescripts of the S. Penitentiaria says: "Unless the rescript of the S. Penitentiaria ordains otherwise, a dispensation from an occult impediment, granted in the non-sacramntal forum, should be annotated in the book, which according to can. 379 must be diligently kept in the secret archives of the Curia, and no other dispensation for the external forum is necessary, even though the occult impediment should become public afterwards. Another dispensation is how-

---

[35] St. Alph. VI, no. 902; Gennari, p, 244; Wernz, no. 62; Gasparri, no. 438.

[36] Wernz, no. 619, note 87.

[37] Wernz, no. 618, note 79; Reiff. App. no. 45; Sanchez, II disp. 40, no. 11; D'Annibale, p. 111 par. 490 no. 26.

[38] Gasparri, no. 441.

ever necessary if the dispensation has been only granted in the sacramental forum." "The Ordinaries should follow this practice, when granting dispensations and thus avoid many difficulties.

If the impediment, without being as yet public, is known to the Bishop in the external forum, he must refrain from enjoining separation and from instituting proceedings against marriage, if he knows by secret but legimate testimony that a dispensation has been granted in the sacramental forum, for instance, through a statement made by the confessor, who with the permission of the penitent has informed the Ordinary of the fact.[39] Even, when the impediment has become public, the dispensation for the internal forum, which is known to have been asked for "must be considered as valid in the external forum, and the ecclesiastical judge is neither bound nor able to take judicial cognizance of the impediment in question, unless it has been brought before him in due form of law."[40]

In these ordinary faculties are included the powers to revalidate a dispensation obtained from Rome, but invalid on account of some occult defect, when the case demands immediate attention and no new dispensation can be procured. These faculties include the power of cumulating since this faculty is always enjoyed by an Ordinary, when he dispenses in virtue of ordinary or delegated powers.[41]

These ordinary faculties always include the power of legitimating the children excepting the adulterine and the sacrilegious, which require a special rescript from the Pope.[42] The legitimation has reference to both the unborn and those already born (can. 1051). These faculties also contain the power to absolve from censures, if there are any, in order that the dispensation may take effect (can. 66, 3).[43]

Voluntary powers, either ordinary or delegated, are not suspended, when the case has been brought before a superior, disregarding the inferior. But once the case is brought before the superior, the inferior should not interfere, except in urgent cases, in which circumstances the superior must be notified (can. 204 and 1048). Applying this to Ordinaries, canon 1048 states: Ordinaries may not use the powers they may have when a dispensa-

[39] Feije, De imp. no. 693. De Smet, no. 346.

[40] S. Poenitentiaria July 29, 1891; Sabetti-Barrett, no. 919 ed. 22. See also canon 202.

[41] Sanchez, lib. II disp. 40, n. 6. Canon 1049.

[42] S. Poenitent. July 1, 1859; S. C. Inq. July 8, 1903; Gasparri, n. 471.

[43] S. Poenitent. July 1, 1859; Gasparri, no. 471, ed. 111.

tion has been asked from the Holy See, except in cases of urgent necessity.

In granting dispensations by ordinary powers it is not absolutely necessary to follow the style of the Curia, but by far the best method to employ.[44]

Ordinary jurisdiction is that, which is attached to the office by law (can. 197). Any one, who enjoys ordinary powers, may delegate them to others, either totally or in part, unless the law expressly forbids this (can. 199). What a person can do of his own right, that he can do through others(Reg. 69). Hence Ordinaries can delegate all those who are free from defects that bar the reception of jurisdiction. These defects arise either from nature, as deafness, insanity, age etc. or from law, as excommunication (can. 2265), interdict (can. 2275), suspension (2283) and infamy (can. 2294).[45] Ordinary jurisdiction is attached to the office itself, hence a mere appointment to a person, having such jurisdiction joined to it, includes the grant of ordinary powers. As it is a favor to the holder of office, it does not cease at the death of the giver. Neither is it lost by renunciation, privation, removal, translation of the granter (can. 183). It ceases however by loss of office and is suspended during the time of an appeal in suspensivo (can. 208).

These powers cannot be exercised by one, who is excommunicated, suspended, interdicted or infamous in the sense of the canons: 2264, 2275, 2294. Ordinary jurisdiction, or jurisdiction granted for all causes, permits of a wide interpretation (can. 200).

The power of jurisdiction can only be exercised towards subjects, but unless the law makes special provisions, voluntary jurisdiction of which we are speaking, may be exercised in one's own favor, or when outside of the territory, or towards subjects outside of the territory (can. 201). When granting any powers of ordinary jurisdiction to priests or confessors it is well to specify them. General commission as "I grant you all faculties and jurisdiction that I have" is not sufficient. As a rule the delegation should be made in writing and the most important faculties mentioned to remove all anxiety.[46]

---

[44] S. P. June 2, 1891; Putzer, p. 15-38; Gasparri, n. 445; Wernz, n. 620, note 95.

[45] Tunton, p. 279.

[46] Reiff. App. n. 35; Schmalzgr. IV, tit. XVI, n. 75; Sanchez, II disp. 40 n. 14.

CHAPTER VII

Dispensations and Absolutions Granted by Priests in Virtue of Ordinary Powers

Anterior to the New Code, no priest had ordinary powers to dispense either in virtue of his office, presumed or tacit consent of the Church, or by custom. This discipline has now been changed and we shall indicate in this chapter, what powers are enjoyed (1) by parish priests, (2) simple priests and (3) confessors.

1. The parish priest, says canon 83, cannot dispense from the common, nor the particular law, unless this power has been expressly granted him. Such powers have been conceded to him in regard to feast-days and fast and abstinence. In particular cases and for just reasons he can dispense his subjects, either the individual or the family, even outside of his territory and strangers within his territory, from the observance of feast-days, fast and abstinence or either (can. 1245).

POWERS IN IMMINENT DANGER OF DEATH

The parish priest has the same powers that the Ordinaries enjoy, when certain circumstances arise and no recourse to the Ordinary is possible. Hence he can dispense: (1) *Urgente mortis periculo.* No matter from what cause this danger arises; (2) *ad consulendum conscientiae.* This condition is fulfilled, when the person is bound to marry, e. g. because he cannot otherwise remove the proximate occasion of sin, or even "when the sickness has occasioned his accomplice (or her family) a material loss, which according to the law of the country, can be more readily repaired if he leaves a widow behind him, and the case in which a marriage would put an end to an inveterate family quarrel or prevent a patrimony from being turned to bad use" would be sufficient reason to grant the dispensation.[1]

3. "*Pro casibus in quibus ne loci quidem Ordinarius adire possit.*" The reason why no delegation can be had, may be danger of death or other valid motives, like the safeguard of some secrets. The necessary time is wanting even, when telegraphic or telephonic communication with the Ordinary is possible, but

[1] Vermeersch, Ne temere, n. 73; Wernz, no. 617; De Smet, n. 369.

not when an registered letter could be sent and an answer recived. (4) *Tum super forma.* The delegated powers granted to simple priests by Pius X (Ne temere. art. VII) did not explicitly define, whether the parish priest was included.[2] This was definitly decided by the decrees of the S. C. de Sacr. (May 14, 1909, July 29, 1910) where it is stated that parish priests are included.[3] It was formerly held that the priest could not dispense from the prensence of witnesses, not even in danger of death. The code clearly states that parish priests enjoy the faculty to dispense from the formalities of matrimony. Hence, when no witnesses are to be had, they are not needed and the parish priest under these circumstances can assist at a marriage even outside of his territory (can. 1044).

5. *'Tum super omnibus et singulis impedimentis."* This power embraces either forum and dispensation is granted for the external or internal forum according to the nature of the impediment. In these absolute general terms of the Code the power of cumulating is included, because the Church wishes as far as possible to provide for the welfare of the dying.[4] The dispensation for the external forum should be committed to writing. The parish priest is likewise obliged to notify the Ordinary, when a dispensation has been granted in the external forum and enter it in the marriage register (can. 1046). What has been said regarding the other conditions, scandal, consummation of marriage and the necessary promises, must be applied here.

IN CASES OF URGENT NECESSITY

The parish priest enjoys additional powers by law, when everything is in readiness for the nuptials and the marriage cannot be postponed without probable grave danger of evil (can. 1043, 3). With the same conditions and restrictions that bind the Ordinary in such cases, the parish priest can dispense from all impediments from which the Ordinary can dispense, but in *occult cases* only and provided he cannot apply to the Ordinary, or if he did apply, there would be danger of violating a sercet.

The conditions in regard to scandal, mixed religion and disparity of worship are the same as above.

---

[2] Ne temere art. VII; Act. I, 448, II, 650; L. Wouters, Com. in Decret. Ne temere, p. 73; De Smet, n. 369.

[3] Vermeersch, De Relig. Period. V. p. 38; Van der Acker, p. 69; Vogt, p. 158. Against: L. Wouters, p. 70; Ferreres, Les Esp. n. 599 and 617; Leitner, Lehrbuch, p. 484.

[4] L. Wouters, Ne temere, p. 71.

"Sed solum pro casibusoccultis." It is quite evident that this clause has no reference to a private marriage. Does it mean that the parish priest can dispense only from occult impediments? If this were true, the parish priest would have no ordinary power to dispense from impediments, which can be proved in the external forum and hence in many cases would find himself deprived of all powers. If for example two expressed their desire to contract marriage and just before the celebration the priest upon investigation found that they are related but nobody in the place knew of the fact, he could not dispense them, if the impediment can be proved in the external forum. Even though there would be grave danger in delay and it were most difficult to have recourse to the Ordinary, the priest could do nothing. The difficulty would be still greater, if with the impediment of consanguinity, one of the parties were bound by the vow of chastity. An occult case apparently means one, which does not arouse the admiration of the people. The canon cannot mean to exclude a public impediment, which is not known by the community because it would have to be stated. It is certainly not apparent. When speaking of he public impediment, the Code says: "censetur publicum," which indicates that it is presumed to be public. We cannot assume such presumption here and logically the case is occult as long as the people are not aware of an impediment.

One might object saying: if the priest can dispense from occult and public impediments, he has more power than the S. Penitentiaria. This objection was formerly raised by Benedict XIV against the opinion that the Bishop can dispense from an impediment, which is only formally occult.[5] The objection no longer holds since the New Code expressly grants such powers to Ordinaries. Under conditions which obtain in the perplexed case we believe that the priest can also dispense from public impediments provided the case is an occult one.

If an occult case means an occult impediment only, why is this not mentioned? The Pagella, which the S. Penitentiaria grants to Ordinaries and priests expressly states occult impediment. Occult impediment was always mentioned in the faculties formerly given to Bishops in virtue of tacit consent of the Pope.[6] Canon 1043 makes special reference to occult and public impediments and the reason, why canon 1045 reads, "in casibus occultis" is no other than this: By law the priest can dispense from the

---

[5] Wernz, n. 618, note 79; Gasparri, n. 440.

[6] Wernz, n. 618, 619; Gasparri, 440; Putzer, p. 22.

same occult and public impediments from which the Ordinary can dispense, but only when such dispensations do not arouse admiration among the people. When therefore is the case an occult case? The doctrine formerly applied to occult impediments may be here used to advantage. We must consider the number of people, who know of the case, the size of the community and especially the quality of the persons, who have knowledge of the affair. If six in a village, eight or ten in a city are aware of the public impediment, but are friends or relatives of the parties the case could be considered occult. If on the contrary the quality of the person is such that there is grave danger of publicity, the case would have to be considered public and no dispensation could be granted by ordinary powers.[7] In the latter case it is easy to await the dispensation from the Ordinary without disgrace or scandal, since the matter is public. If the priest did dispense, he would rather provoke than avoid scandal.[8]

When the parish priest discovers an impediment just before marriage, the first step to take will be, to investigate of what nature the impediment is. When this is ascertained and the marriage cannot be postponed the following course should be persued. We must first bear in mind the distinction between impediments of natural law, from which no dispensation is granted and those of ecclesiastical law in which the Church dispenses, either with ease, under no circumstance, or seldom.

1. When there is question of a public impediment from which no dispensation is possible and the people are aware of this, no priest can lend his assistance in the matter. If the public impediment is not known to the people, the parish priest may follow the rules laid down below in regard to indispensable occult impediments.

2. A public impediment from which dispensation can be granted: When the people know about the impediment the priest can do nothing, unless he has faculties to dispense, and he must refer the case to the Ordinary.[9] When the case is occult in the sense we have explained, the parish priest simply grants the dispensation, notifies the Ordinary and enters the marriage in the marriage register.

---

[7] Putzer, p. 29; Reiff. App. n. 46; Feije, n. 96; St. Alphonsus, lib. VI IIII; Zitelli, disp. p. 90.

[8] Reiff. App. n. 43; Schmalzgr. IV Decret. t. XVI, n. 82; De Smet, n. 354.

[9] Synod. dioces. Albanensis, p. 11, tit. IX no. 13; Gasparri, no. 247.

3. An occult impediment of the ecclesiastical law, excepting the impediments arising from the Priesthood and affinity in direct line: When both parties are in good faith, the parish priest will assist at the marriage without disturbing their minds and grant the dispensation in virtue of his ordinary powers. If one of the parties knows of the impediment and the other does not, it is no longer necessary to have recourse to the uncertain restrictions, which demanded the celebration of marriage "sub conditione," the subsequent obligation to abstain from the nuptial congress, and the renewal of consent. The parish priest simply dispenses in this case.

The perplexed case proper consisted in this; One of the parties declares to have knowledge of an impediment but cannot inform the other without grave inconvenience, or cannot obtain a dispensation on that day. Authors generally believed that the impediment ceases under such circumstances.[10] In order to show due respect for the law canonists generally demanded that recourse should be had after the marriage to the Ordinary or the S. Penitentiaria to procure a dispensation ad cautelam. Practically these difficulties have now disappeared. The parish priest, in virtue of ordinary powers, can dispense even when both are in bad faith. The priest is obliged however, as in the case of imminent danger of death, to notify the Ordinary of any dispensation granted in the external forum and make a note of it in the marriage register (can. 1046). Supposing however the impediment was purposely concealed by both? Must we apply the rule "nemo ex propria malitia commodum habere debeat"?[11] They are unworthy to receive the sacrament but it will lie with the good judgment of the priest to dispose them and, even if he fails, to prevent greater evil, he will not refuse to grant them a dispensation.[12]

4. An occult indispensable impediment. As a general rule the priest cannot assist at such marriages. If both parties however are in good faith, he may sometimes leave them in good faith, since no one is obliged to impede material loss, when a still greater evil, scandal among the faithful or grave harm, would result. Hence according to a probable opinion, when only

---

[10] D'Ann. p. 111, par. 454; Scavini, vol. III, n. 903; Gury, vol. II, n. 771; Roncaglia, De Matr. XXI q. V. c. Iq. 2; Rossett, n. 2403; Gasparri, n. 249; Gennari, Cons. vol. I consult. 127; St. Alph. lib. VI n. 613; Hom. Ap. XVI et tract. XVIII n. 8; Praxis confess. n. 8 et 84.

[11] Gennari l. c. n. 8.

[12] Gasparri, n. 249.

one or even when both are in bad faith, the priest can assist at such marriages. He must admonish them however, and only in extreme cases is he allowed to comply with their wishes. Such assistance is not intrinsically wrong because he only assists as witness to the invalid and sacrilegious marriage.[13]

What course must the parish priest follow, when this urgent need for a dispensation occurs in regard to contracted marriages? According to many authors the impediment ceases under the circumstances.[14] The old discipline however required good faith in at least one of the parties. In virtue of canon 1045, par. 2, the ordinary faculties of the parish priest extend to the revalidation of contracted marriages providing there is danger in delay and recourse to the Ordinary is difficult.

In occult cases, therefore, the parish priest can dispense from all ecclesiastical impediments except those arising from the Priesthood or affinity in direct line, under the following conditions: (1) Subjects he can dispense everywhere, strangers only within his territory; (2) there is no scandal; (3) the necessary promises have been made; (4) the intervention of the Ordinary cannot easily be obtained; (5) there is danger in delay; (6) or danger of violating secrets.

SIMPLE PRIESTS

An ordinary priest has no power to grant dispensations unless such faculties are especially given to him. The New Code endows even simple priests, who have no parochial rights or jurisdiction, with various powers. In imminent danger of death, every priest in accordance with canon 1098, 2, can validly and licitly assist at a marriage provided: (1) the Ordinary, the parish priest or a delegate cannot be had; (2) the parties wish to set their conscience right or legitimate their children.

Under these conditions any priest can dispense from the formalities of marriage i. e. witnesses, when they cannot be procured, or from territorial limitations. He can likewise dispense from all impediments, occult, public or multiple, except the impediments arising from the Priesthood or affinity in direct line. All that the priest is required to do is to notify the Ordinary about the dispensation granted in the external forum and make the proper annotations in the marriage register (can. 1046). Care must be taken to remove all scandal and to exact the neces-

[13] D'Anniabale, p. 111, par. 462, n. 8. Gasparri, no. 250.

[14] Lehmkuhl, Theol. Mor. II n. 826; Ballerini Palmieri, VI, n. 207; Noldin, n. 656.

sary promises, when a dispensation is granted from the impediment of mixed religion or disparity of worship. For explanation of the various conditions, we refer to what has been said above. Canon 1098 says *alius sacerdos:* Since it does not specify the quality of the priest, the marriage is valid and licit before any priest whatever, even before one who is suspended or excommunicated by name and deprived of all delegation.[15] Any dispensations that he may grant are valid and licit.

In order to contract marriage validly without the presence of the priest, it is required: (1) that there be grave inconvenience in sending for or in going to the competent priest, i. e., parish priest or the delegate:[16] (2) that this state of affairs as prudently forseen, will last for a month.[17] Canon 1098 says if another priest can be had, he must assist at the marriage, though the marriage would be valid with only two witnesses.

Under these circumstances, when all preparations have been made for the marriage, and it cannot be postponed without probable grave peril of evil, any priest enjoys the same powers that the parish priest has, with the conditions and restrictions mentioned. The same powers also extend to contracted marriages.

These powers which are granted to ordinary priests for marriages under peculiar circumstances are new and clearly indicate how well the Church provides for the welfare of all the faithful.

CONFESSORS

a) In regard to dispensations in imminent danger of death and when all preparations have been made for the marriage, the confessors have the same powers that the parish priest has, with this one important exception. According to canon 1044 the confessor can dispense only in the internal forum, and then only in the sacramental forum. Outside of confession the confessor can do nothing, but in confession he can grant the dispensations mentioned even though the parties are unworthy to receive absolution. As we shall explain later, it is the duty of the confessor to try to dispose the penitents or, if possible, to postpone the absolution and dispensation, but according to a decision of the S. Pen-

[15] De Smet, n. 68; Vermeersch, Ne temere, n. 74; Wouters, p. 68.

[16] S. C. C. July 27, 1908; Ojetti, Anal. eccl. 190, p. 341; De Smet, n. 69.

[17] Can. 1098; De Becker, Legislatio Nova. 1908, p. 36; Wouters l. c. p. 75 S. C. de S. Jan. 31, 1916; Sabetti-Barrett, ed. 26, n. 912; Boudinhon, Can. cont. 1910, p. 264; Ferreres, esp. 5 ed. Madrid 1911, n. 806.

itentiaria, 19 May, 1834, a dispensation can be granted even when absolution must be deferred.[18]

The confessor upon the discovery of any public impediment in confession must insist that the parties abstain from marriage until dispensation has been procured, and furthermore he must demand of them to reveal this impediment to their pastor outside of confession. If they refuse to comply with this request, absolution must be refused. If the case is occult, and the parties are ignorant of the impediment, the confessor in most cases will do well to leave them in good faith. When both or when only one of the parties knows that an impediment exists, the confessor simply makes use of his ordinary powers and grants the necessary dispensation. He proceeds the same way in the case of a public impediment which is in fact occult.

When the impediment is an indispensable one or one from which no dispensation is granted, as for instance affinity in direct line, and the parties are in good faith they may be left in good faith, unless grave scandal would follow. If the penitent knows that in such cases no dispensation is granted, the confessor must tell him that nothing can be done.[19] It is well to remember that the parish priest, who is at the same time the confessor, must always assist at the marriage, if he knows only from confession that the parties are unworthy.

As the ordinary faculties of the parish priest, under certain circumstances, extend to revalidation of contracted marriages, so too the law accords the same right to confessors. In occult cases, and in the sacramental forum, the confessor can dispense from all ecclesiastical impediments from which the Ordinary can dispense in such cases, but with the following conditions: (1) his parishioners everywhere and strangers within his territory; (2) that there be no scandal; (3) the necessary assurances are given; (4) recourse to the Ordinary is difficult; (5) there is danger in delay; (6) or danger of violating some secret. No records are kept of these dispensations, because they are of no value for the external forum.

b) Absolutions from reserved cases.

During the time in which the faithful are obliged to make their Easter duty, every parish priest is competent to absolve from all episcopal reservations. The missionaries enjoy the same powers during the time of the mission (can. 899, 3).

---

[18] Gasparri, no. 412.

[19] Gasparri, n. 246.

Every reservation ceases for the sick, who wish to confess and cannot leave the house, and for those who go to confession as a preparation for marriage. The reservation ceases even when the lawful superior has refused the faculty to absolve in a certain case, or when in the prudent judgment of the confessor the power to absolve cannot be obtained without grave inconvenience on the part of the penitent, or when there is danger of violating the seal of confession. Reserved cases do not bind when the delinquent has left the territory, even though he went elsewhere for the purpose of obtaining absolution (can. 900). The censure, however, inflicted "*ab homine*" bind the penitent everywhere (can. 2247, 2).

c) Absolution from censure.

Every priest can absolve those who are in danger of death from any sins or censures. "It has been piously held by the Church of God that there is no reservation in regard to those who are in danger of death. In order that none may perish, every priest can absolve penitents from any sins or censures."[20] The New Code reiterates the same in these words: Every priest, even those not approved to hear confessions, can absolve any penitent who is in danger of death from every kind of sin or censure, no matter how notorious or reserved, even when another competent priest is present (can. 882). There is one exception. Absolution of the accomplice (in peccato turpi) is valid when there is danger of death, but illicit except in cases of necessity (can. 884).

All those, who when in danger of death, have been absolved from censure, reserved by man or in a special manner by the Apostolic See, must after recovery and under pain of relapse, have recourse to the one who inflicted the censure, if it is a censure "*ab homine,*" or to the S. Penitentiaria, the Bishop, or any one with faculties, if it is a censure "*a iure*" (can. 2252). The same powers are granted to confessors in cases of urgent necessity.[21] Any confessor can absolve from reserved cases in the sacramental forum under these conditions: (1) that the case be urgent, (2) that censures latae sententiae cannot be endured without grave danger of scandal, infamy, or (3) that it be difficult for the penitent to remain in the state of mortal sin until provision has been made by the competent superior. The penitent, under pain

---

[20] Concil. Trid. sess. 14, c. 7.

[21] Noldin, n. 431, ed. VI. Powers of confessors to dispense from vindictive penalties are similar to these (can. 2290). Ignorance of reservation (can. 2247): For special powers of confessors in regard to irregularities see canon 990.

of relapse, must take upon himself the obligation to have recourse within a month by letter, or through the confessor if possible without grave inconvenience, to the S. Penitentiaria, Bishop, or another superior having faculties, by whose decisions he must abide (can. 2254).

To avoid these obligations, the penitent may choose another confessor, who has the necessary faculties, confess his sins, at least the crime to which the censure is attached and follow his commands (can. 2254, 2). If in an extraordinary case approach to the superior is morally impossible, the confessor can grant absolution without imposing the obligation to have recourse, excepting the censure attached to the crime of absolving an accomplice (can. 2254, 3). The confessor must not omit to enjoin all that is rejuired by law, impose a salutary penance and satisfaction for the censure. The penitent is also warned that unless he fulfills the penance and gives satisfaction within the limited time, he relapses into the same censure. (can. 2254, 3).

CHAPTER VIII

Dispensations and Absolutions Granted in Virtue of Delegated Faculties

Besides the ordinary powers, which we have treated, Ordinaries have delegated powers varying with the extent of the faculties granted them by favor of the Holy See. It will suffice merely to indicate the most important ones, because the changes of the New Code make a total or partial remodelling of the different formulas imperative.

They are divided into ordinary and extraordinary faculties. The ordinary faculties are distinguished with Roman numerals e. g. Form I, Form II, the extraordinary faculties with capital letters, Form C. F. E. The grant of ordinary faculties varies in different countries; that of the extraordinary faculties depends upon the need. In England and Scotland the Bishops have Form II, in Ireland F. VI, in U. S. and Canada F. I. and T.[1] According to Normae pec. (c. VII art. VI n. 3) they can no longer be granted by the S. C. P. F. except to those countries and peoples under its direct jurisdiction, but they have been temporarily renewed and prolonged by the Cong. of the Consistory and are still in force.

The Congregation of the Discipline of the Sacraments also grants quinquennial faculties. They relate both to contracted marriages and marriages to be contracted and include the faculty of cumulating.[2] The Holy Office bestows its faculties to dispense from the impediments of mixed religion and disparity of worship for a limited number of cases or for a definite period.

The faculties mentioned are chiefly for the external forum. The S. Penitentiaria gives quinquennial faculties for the internal forum, to dispense from various impediemnts and to absolve from numerous censures.[3]

EXPLANATION OF POWERS

Delegated faculties granted either in perpetuum, for a definite time or for a certain number of cases, are considered to be

[1] Taunton, p. 522.

[2] Bargilliat, p. 476, n. 584 ed. 30.

[3] Bargilliat, n. 487; F. Capello, De Cur. Ro. Pustet, 1911, p. 363.

privileges "*praeter jus*" (can. 66) and hence admit a wide interpretation, but all expansive or arbitrary explanation is prohibited. Canon 200 says: ordinary jurisdiction and jurisdiction for the universality of cases can be interpreted widely all other jurisdiction must be taken strictly. When there is question of a dispensation according to canon 50, or a single case, strict interpretation is always demanded (can. 85). Hence nothing more can be inferred from them except that which the faculties explicitly or implicitly contain. They do include those powers however, which are necessary for the exercise of the faculties (can. 66). The faculty to dispense includes the power to absolve from censure but only in order that the dispensation may take effect.[4] A faculty to dispense, when a marriage is to be contracted, cannot be used for a marriage already contracted. Faculties to dispense in favor of converts, cannot be extended to Catholics.[5] Whosoever claims that he has faculties to dispense, has the obligation to prove his claim in case of doubt (can. 200).

The general faculty, not that for a particular case, to dispense from diriment impediments, includes ipso facto the power of legitimating the children, excepting the sacrilegious and adulterine.[6] The dispensation granted for the impediment of affinity does not extend to the impediment of public decency, since according to the Code, there is no connection between the two.[7] When the indult contains no restrictive clauses, dispensation can be granted even though both parties have the same impediment, or the impediment, arising from various cause, is multiple.[8]

The faculty of cumulating gave rise to many difficulties in the past. It was not necessary in the following cases: (1) When an impediment public by its nature, occurred simultaneously with another impediment occult or of the internal forum."[9] (2) When several occult impediments were present.[10] (3) When the degrees were multiple. [11]

When the Ordinary dispensed in virtue of delegated powers, he could not dispense the same person from various public impediments, unless he had expressly obtained such faculties from

[4] Gasparri, n. 471; can. 200.

[5] Wernz, n. 621, note 101.

[6] S. P. July 1, 1859; S. C. O. July 8, 1903; Gasparri, 471; can. 1051.

[7] Wernz, n. 622; Gasparri, n. 465; Can. 97, 1078.

[8] Wernz, n. 622; Gasparri, n. 465; Can. 1049.

[9] S. C. S. O. 31 mar. 1872; Aug. 18, 1897.

[10] Sanchez, L. II D. 40. no. 6; Genarri, Cons. 12, cons. 107, n. 7.

[11] S. Penitentiaria Apr. 20, 1883; Gasparri, n. 465.

the Apostolic See.[12] The faculty of cumulating was always required, when a diriment impediment occurred with a prohibitive impediment reserved to the Pope.[13] Gasparri[14] plainly states that, according to various decisions of the S. Penitentiaria, Propaganda and the Holy Office, the faculty of cumulating must be especially mentioned, if it should comprehend several impediments in the same case. The faculty of cumulating could not be used in conjunction with the power of revalidating marriages in radice. A special concession from the Holy See was required for this.[15]

All this, excepting the power of revalidating "in radice," has only historical value now. The Code (can. 1049) says: Any one who has a general indult to dispense from various kinds of impediments, either diriment or prohibitive, can dispense from these impediments, even public impediments, when they occur in the same case.

DELEGATION AND SUBDELEGATION

Formerly the question was agitated; can a delegate subdelegate his powers, when no such express permission is given?[16] The S. C. S. O. (Dec. 17, 1898) to the question: "Can a Bishop without special permission subdelegate to his V. G. or to other ecclesiastics, generally, or at least in a particular case, the temporary powers delegated to him by the Holy See"? replied "*affirmative*," provided this is not forbidden in the indult, and the faculty of subdelegating is not there restricted to certain persons only, for in that case the tenor of the rescript must be strictly observed." The discipline has not been altered very much by the New Code. The Bishops are the executors of the papal rescripts and therefore enjoy full powers of subdelegation (can. 57).

The power of ordinary or delegated jurisdiction can be subdelegated either for a particular case or habitually, unless the power is restricted to a certain person or subdelegation is prohibited. The power of jurisdiction for the universality of cases can be subdelegated for particular cases (can. 199). Those who are delegated by the Holy See can subdelegate others habitually or for a particular instance, unless they be appointed to deal with

---

[12] S. C. S. O. May 18, 1869; July 2, 1884; S. Penitent. Jan. 18, 1883.

[13] S. C. S. O. Sep. 12, 1888; Aug. 18, 1879; Wernz n. 622, note 108.

[14] Gasparri, n. 465.

[15] Wernz, 622; Gasparri, 467.

[16] Wernz, n. 622, note 104; Gasparri, n. 448, 1132; Sanchez, lib. III D. 31.

matters personally or subdelegation be prohibited (can. 199). Preparatory acts may always be committed to another, even when subdelegation is prohibited e. g. verifying facts in a case. Formerly when faculties were granted to Bishops the V. G. could not use the faculties unless the Bishop delegated him. Now the V. G. is implicitly included, when the Holy See grants faculties to the Bishop (can. 66). A subdelegate has no power to delegate unless especially permitted to do so (can. 199).

All those, who are worthy and capable of ecclesiastical jurisdiction can be chosen as delegates.[17] We have mentioned the requisites, when speaking of the ordinary powers. The faculties granted by the S. Penitentiaria can be subdelegated; "to the Canon Penitentiary and the Deans for the forum of conscience and in confession alone, but habitually if so desired; to other confessors, when they apply in a particular case or even for a definite term."[18]

The so-called Propaganda faculties can be subdelegated wholly or in part as the case may be and the rescripts indicate. Unless the nature of the case demands it or the law makes other provisions, voluntary jurisdiction may be exercised in one's own interest. A delegate having faculties to dispense, can make use of this power to dispense himself. He may exercise his power even outside of his territory in favor of those within his domain. Subjects of the delegate, who are outside of their territory are not excluded from the scope of voluntary jurisdiction (can. 201). Delegates who exceed their powers in regard to persons or matters, render the faculties null and void for that particular case. The delegate is free however to employ his own method of procedure unless the method is prescribed also (can. 203).

Delegated faculties cannot be extended to different territories or forums, to a larger number of cases or impediments. They are void after the time limit has elapsed unless this is especially permitted. Thus the "Pagella" of the S. Penitentiaria ratifies all absolutions and dispensations which are granted through forgetfulness or inadvertance, when the time limit allotted by the faculties has expired.[19] The New Code (can. 207, 2) applies this rule to the internal forum in general, stating: When there is question of powers for the internal forum, the concession granted by inattention, after the limited period has elapsed or the number of cases in exhausted, is valid.

---

[17] X. cap. 2, De judic. Cap. 41 De off. deleg. Bargilliat, no. 238.

[18] Pagella S. Penitent. Introduction.

[19] Pagella S. Penitent. in fine.

Faculties which the Holy See habitually grants to Bishops or Ordinaries are not suspended nor do they cease at their death or cessation of office but pass to their successors.[20] Hence at the death of the Bishop the faculties pass to the Vicar Capitular or the Administrator and then to the new Bishop even in a case of "*res non integra.*"

Delegated faculties cease: by the completion of the business, by lapse of a fixed period, when the limited number of cases has been exhausted, by cessation of the final cause, by revocation of the delegator made known to the delegate, by renunciation of the delegate made known and accepted by the delegator.[21] It does not cease by cessation of office of the delegator unless the rescript contains a special clause to that effect or unless the rescript is given in favor of particular persons mentioned and the "res is adhuc integra" (can. 207). An exception to this canon has been mentioned namely: an inadvertent act placed in the internal forum, when the time limit has elapsed or the number of cases has been exhausted, is valid. The rule given by the canon 209 deserves special mention. The Church supplies the jurisdiction both for the external and the internal forum, when there is question of common error or a positive and probable doubt as to the law or fact. The Church does not encourage culpable ignorance or negligence, but in her solicitude for the welfare of souls, she relaxes her laws and remedies the defects of human frailty.

---

[20] S. C. S. O. Feb. 20, 1888, Nov. 24, 1897.

[21] Cap. 7, de procurator. in 6to; Bargilliat, no. 425 sq.; Gasparri, n. 429; Wernz, n. 622; Cf. ex gr. cap, ult. De Rescriptis in 6to.

CHAPTER IX

How to Apply for Dispensations

It is the sacred duty of the clergy to know how to answer questions of conscience and solve difficulties relating to the welfare of souls. The confessor must be acquainted at least in a general way with the S. Penitentiaria and be able to judge, in which cases this Sacred Tribunal is competent to act and how to apply for favors. The parish priest will be called upon to act in many cases and hence will do well to learn how to expedite matters to the satisfaction of all concerned.

Formulas for absolutions, commutations, condonations are found in numerous authors and need not be mentioned here.[1] With regard to matrimonial dispensations, matters are more complicated and require a closer study. The first step to take will be to investigate to what forum the impediment belongs. When this has been ascertained according to the rules we have pointed out, the parish priest or the simple priest takes up the matter for the external forum, the confessor looks to the forum of conscience. When priests or confessors find that they have no faculties to dispense in a particular case, they may direct the petitioner to apply elsewhere, but when this is not practical, the zealous priest will not refuse to lend his assistance.

In cases of imminent danger of death or urgent necessity the priest will not hesitate to make use of the extensive faculties granted him by the New Code as pointed out above. When the parish priest or confessor discovers an impediment which does not demand immediate solution, they must first investigate the nature of it and the causes for dispensation. If the impediment is such that the Holy See alone is competent in the matter, the priest and confessor will do well to inform themselves to whom application must be made. The S. C. de Sacram. dispenses from public impediments, the S. Penitentiaria from the occult, the S. C. S. O. from those concerning faith, the S. C. de P. F. from all impediments for her subjects, the S. C. Reg. from the vow of chastity taken in religion, and the S. C. Eccl. Oriental. for the Orientals.

---

[1] Capello, De Cur. Rom. Pustet 1913.

GENERAL RULE

The confessor or parish priest either for the external or for the internal forum should apply directly to the Ordinary, since the Holy See generally receives petitions and grants favor through the agency of the Ordinary. For the internal forum recourse is sometimes had to the Holy See through the agency of the confessor. The confessor is invariably called upon to apply in the name of the petitioners, when the secrecy of the confession demands this, but when this is not the case the best method will be to send the letter to the Ordinary, who will draw up the supplica and forward it to Rome if necessary.

As a rule the faithful do not apply for dispensations themselves, though they are authorized to do so. Before the constitution "Sapienti consilio" private persons could not apply to the S. Congregation except to the S. Penitentiaria. Even Bishops were obliged to employ an agent. Today the rule is that all the faithful have free recourse to the Holy See and only special grants must be accompanied by commendatory letters of the Ordinary.[2] Even a third party may ask for the dispensation without the knowledge of the parties affected by the impediment. The dispensation would be valid before the acceptance but of course could not be granted against the will of the recipient.[3]

Ordinaries are under no obligation to employ agents but are free to do so. If the Ordinary employs a permanent agent or procurator in Rome, the agent for the legitimate exercise of his office must have his name inscribed in the official catalogue of procurators. This is not necessary when the agent is engaged for a particular case only.[4]

Language: Since the Constitution "Sapienti consilio," Latin, Italian, French, English, Spanish, German, Portuguese can be used in drawing up the supplica. Latin being the language of the Church is especially recommended, but the others may be employed.[5] Recourse to the S. Penitentiaria is even easier. Any language either those mentioned or any modern tongue may be used, only when the petitioners write in their own language, they should employ the Latin characters.[6] Everybody, lay or ecclesiastical, men or women, in person or through the agency of others,

---

[2] Capello, vol. I, p. 43.

[3] Canon 37; Gasparri, n. 378.

[4] Normae com. cap. X n. 1; cap. IX n. 1, 3; Sabetti-Barrett, n. 926,946.

[5] Norm. pec. Vi. n. 5; S. C. de P. F. May 18, 1896.

[6] Capello, p. 359, vol. I; S. C. de P. F. Sep. 29, 1868.

may write and apply to the S. Penitentiaria. Only those who are excommunicated, suspended or interdicted after a declaratory or condemnatory sentence, cannot validly obtain rescripts unless the clause of absolution is attached to the grant.[7]

If the confessor in writing to Rome does employ an agent, the following monitum of the S. Penitentiaria must be strictly observed: "Ceterum si opera alicuius procuratoris in alma Urbe uti velint, litteras obsignatas praelaudato Cardinali Poenitentiario Maiori tradendas suppressis nomnibus ad ipsum procuratorem transmittere quidem poterunt, ast memoratos casus S. Poenitentiariae proponendos nunquam aut nullimodo narrare seu manifestare audeant."[8]

What method must be followed, when a dispensation is to be obtained from two impediments the one public the other occult?

When two impediments, the one public the other occult, occur in the same case, it is important to know how to proceed. Two petitions or supplica must be drawn up, one for the external forum, another for the internal forum. They are then sent to the S. C. de Sacram. and the S. Penitentiaria respectively.[9] The S. Penitentiaria dispenses only from occult impediments and the dispensation from occult impediments, granted in the sacramental forum, is of no value in the external forum though the marriage is valid. Bargilliat states: "if an occult impediment from which the S. Penitentiaria has dispensed, becomes public, another dispensation must be applied for in the S. C. de Sacram. for the external forum, otherwise the children of such marriages would be reputed illegitimate, though the marriage would be valid in the forum of conscience.[10] This is only partly true now since canon 1047 referring to rescripts of the S. Penitentiaria states: "Unless the rescript of the S. Penitentiaria ordains otherwise, a dispensation from an occult impediment, granted in the non-sacramental forum, should be annotated in the book, which according to can. 379 must be diligently kept in the secret archives of the Curia, and no other dispensation for the external forum is necessary, even though the occult impediment should become public afterwards. Another dispensation is however necessary, if the dispensation has been granted only in the sacramental forum."

---

[7] Canons 2275, 2265, 2283.

[8] Act. S. Sed. vol. VII, p. 208; Wernz, n. 632, note 163.

[9] Gasparri, no. 31.

[10] Bargilliat, ed. 30, no. 438, b.

The discipline of the Church requires that all impediments should be named and removed at the same time. To mention the occult impediment however in the external forum, would injure the reputation of the penitent, and on the other hand a public impediment cannot be removed in the internal forum. This is one of the reasons, why a dispensation is asked from the public impediment in the external forum, but it is secretly null because of the occult impediment. Other reasons are: the more impediments there are in a case, the more difficult it is to obtain dispensation and when a dispensation is granted the clause "*si aliud non obstat*" is always understood.[11] When therefore the dispensation from the occult impediment is granted in the internal forum, the dispensation of the external forum for the public impediment is revalidated provided it has been mentioned in the internal forum. In other words the S. Penitentiaria really grants the dispensation from both impediments and the other Congregation merely provides proofs for the external forum.[12]

Hence the public impediment is named and all the particulars for the external forum in this forum, but nothing is mentioned regarding the occult impediment. In the second petition, which is sent to the S. Penitentiaria mention is made at once of the occult impediment and of the public impediment, signifying that a dispensation has been granted or asked for from this latter in the external forum. Is it allowed to apply to the S. Penitentiaria first and to the S. C. de Sacram. afterwards? According to some authors this is permitted.[13] But they also mention that, when this is done, the dispensation from the occult is not granted until the public impediment has been removed and hence practically coincide with our opinion.

In whose name is the petition drawn up?

In the name of both parties, when they are both Catholics, only in the name of the Catholic party if the other is not a Catholic. In the name of one alone if the impediment affects one or if being common to both, it arises from the delinquency of one.[14]

---

[11] Reiff. App. no. 152; Sanchez, lib. VIII. disp. 23, n. 2; Schmalzgr. L. IV, n. 176.

[12] De Smet, n. 384; Gasparri, n. 246; Wernz, n. 633; Ojetti, Syn. 2383.

[13] Gasparri, n. 346; Gutier, c. 123; Sanchez, L. VIII d. 23, n. 7; Schmalzgr. lib. IV tit. XVI n. 176.

[14] Sabetti-Barrett, n. 925; Wernz, n. 632, note 160.

THE FORM OF THE SUPPLICA

Formerly according to the Instruction of the S. C. de P. F. (May 9, 1877): "if even unwittingly the truth was concealed or a false statement made, the dispensation was void." There are two exceptions to this rule. Any rescript which has the clause "Motu proprio" attached is valid even if the whole truth is not told, providing that at least one of the final causes be true (can. 45). The second exception mentioned in canon 1054 has reference to minor impediments. The dispensation granted for minor impediments is not vitiated by the omission of truth or the assertion of falsehood and is valid even though the final cause be false.

The petition is addressed: "All Eminentissimo Cardinale Penitenziere Magiore—Palazzo del S. Officio—Roma. The heading of the letter is: Beatissime Pater or Eminentissime Princeps or Eminentissime Domine.

The letter contains three parts: the impediments, the causes for dispensation and the request or petition for dispensation.

1. In the supplica directed to the S. Penitentiaria, everything likely to make known the identity of the petitioners must be omitted. The names must be replaced by fictitious names such as Titius etc.

2. To mention the age and the condition of the petitioners or their religion is not required for validity.

3. When the confessor writes directly to the S. Penitentiaria for a dispensation in the forum of conscience only, there is no obligation to mention the diocese.

4. The exact species of the impediment: Whether it is consanguinity or affinity, public decency from an invalid marriage or notorious concubinage; for the impediment of crime, whether it arises from conjugicide with promise of marriage, from conjudicide with adultery or merely from adultery with the promise of marriage. Exact species: e. g. in the impediment of the vow of chastity it must be stated, whether it is perpetual chastity, or a vow of entering an order, or not to marry.[15]

Error in the species formerly invalidated the dispensation.[16] Canon 1052 has made a change in this. Dispensation granted from the impediments of consanguinity and affinity in some degree is valid, although another impediment of the same species, in an equal or an inferior degree, has been concealed. Does this

---

[15] Gasparri, n. 384.

[16] Reiff. App. n. 150; Schmalzgr. lib. IV, tit. XVI, n. 157; Gasparri, n. 384.

mean that a major impediment can be concealed without invalidating the dispensation? Is for instance a dispensation from the second degree of consanguinity valid, though the fact of multiple consanguinity of the same or an inferior degree has been intentionally omitted? An affirmative answer to the preceding questions seems to be the only correct interpretation. The Style of the Curia, which demanded that all impediments, simple or multiple must be mentioned for validity, will have to conform to this canon. Canon 1054 has done away with difficulties concerning obreption or subreption in regard to dispensation from minor impediments.

When an impediment is given as doubtful although it is certain, the dispensation is valid though illicit, because the tacit condition "if there is an impediment" is always understood.[17]

The impediment of affinity arising from illicit intercourse no longer exists, but marriage is never permitted when there is doubt that the parties are blood-relatives in some degree direct line or in the first degree collateral line (can. 1076, 3). In the impediment of public decency the origin line and degree must be given according to canon 1078. Spiritual relationship as an impediment is contracted only through Baptism and by the minister, sponsors and the one baptized. It is not necessary to indicate the number of children unless the impediment is thereby rendered multiple.[18].

5. The degree of consanguinity or of affinity or of public decency, whether it is simple or mixed, not only the remoter degree but also the nearer. The line, whether direct or collateral, likewise if the petitioners are connected by a double tie of consanguinity on the father's side and on the mother's side. Hence, when instead of the nearer degree, the remoter is mentioned the dispensation is certainly invalid. According to some authors the dispensation is also invalid, when a nearer degree is put down instead of the remoter.[19] The practice followed by the S. Penitentiaria considered the dispensation invalid, when the nearer degree was given for the remoter. Other Congregations accepted the more lenient opinion of many authors.[20] The controversy on this matter is now settled by canon 1052. The dispensation granted from the impediments of consanguinity or affinity in

[17] Sanchez, lib. VIII, disp. XXXI n. 40.

[18] Reiff. App. n. 267; Schmalzgr. IV, tit. XXVI, n. 169. Canon 1079, 768.

[19] Gasparri, n. 385.

[20] Wernz, n. 634, note 177; Reiff. App. n. 166; Sanchez, L. VIII, disp. 24, n. 17. Schmalzgr., L. IV, tit. 16, n. 192.

some degree, is valid even if an error in regard to the degree has slipped in the petition or concession of the dispensation, provided the error regards the remoter degree.

When the first degree is in question, the sex should be mentioned, since it is more difficult to obtain dispensation for a nephew to marry his aunt, than for an uncle to marry his niece, but it is not required for validity.[21]

6. The number of impediments must be mentioned e. g. if the consanguinity or affinity is twofold or multiple; if to the consanguinity is joined affinity or any other impediment, whether diriment or prohibitive. Formerly if the multiplicity e. g. of consanguinity of affinity was not mentioned, the dispensation was void.[22] We have seen under number 4 that the dispensation is valid, although another impediment of the same species, in an equal or an inferior degree, has been concealed (can. 1052).

7. The various circumstances, that is to say, whether the marriage is contracted or to be contracted, whether the Banns have been published and the form enjoined by the Council of Trent, Ne temere, or the New Code observed, must be mentioned but for licitness only. It is not necessary for validity to mention that civil marriage was contracted in order to obtain a dispensation more easily.[23] Neither is it necessary to state that a Catholic marriage was contracted to procure dispensation more easily as seen by an answer of the S. Penitentiaria (3 July, 1890).

No one should ask a favor from another Ordinary that has been denied him by his own Ordinary, without mentioning the fact that the petition was refused. When such refusal is mentioned the Ordinary should not grant the favor without having obtained the reasons from the proper Ordinary why the favor was not granted (can. 44). A petition rejected by the Vicar General is invalidly asked from the Bishop unless mention is made of the fact that the favor was refused; if however the petition was refused by the Bishop, it cannot be validly granted by the Vicar General without the consent of the Bishop, even though the refusal was mentioned (can. 44). The S. Penitentiaria can grant dispensations that have been rejected by other Congregations in virtue of canon 43 as we have seen. In the first paragraph of canon 44, where the two Ordinaries are concerned, there is merely a question of licitness. If the second Ordinary should grant the rescript, which was refused by the first and the fact was not men-

[21] Gasparri, n. 385. Feije, n. 703.
[22] Benedict XIV, "Etsi" Sep. 30, 1755; S. C. S. O. Mar. 11, 1896.
[23] Cf. S. Penitentiaria Apr. 18, 1831; Scherer, p. 471, note 84.

tioned, the rescript would be illicit but valid. The second paragraph of canon 44 contains an invalidating law, which renders the contrary act null and void.

Formerly a dispensation was null, not only when the fact of incestuous intercourse was omitted, or the intention of obtaining a dispensation more easily, but also, when after granting dispensation, the parties had been guilty of incest or had repeated the offence mentioned in the supplica, before marriage. According to a provision made by the S. C. S. O. (25 June, 1885), and 18 Mar., 1891) matrimonial dispensations are valid even if the intercourse or the intention of obtaining the dispensation more easily, have not been mentioned.[24]

To avoid all difficulties and danger of omissions it is well to attach the geneological tree and then, even though one is not aware of all the impediments existing in the case, the dispensation will cover all.[25]

Lastly the petition must contain the legitimate causes; this belongs to the substance of the dispensation and is required for validity.

EXPENSES AND TAXES

The S. Penitentiaria, as we have seen (Benedict XIV Const. "In Apostolicae," 13 Apr., 1744, par. 22), granted dispensations in the external forum as it does now exclusively for the internal forum, entirely free of charge and demands neither taxes nor componenda. When applying directly to the S. Tribunal, absolutely nothing is required unless the petitioners are willing to defray the postage, which is merely a just compensation. Agents do not exact nor refuse taxes. Their remuneration is not determined but practice allows them five francs or more according to the labor.[26] When an agent is employed a legitimate compensation is no more than just, but the sum does not exceed the expenses for postage and a little above (3 libellae 60 cents). Even this is not required, when the petitioners are destitute.[27]

The Ordinaries generally observe the Style of the Curia and dispense gratuitously for the internal forum. When the Ordinary dispenses in virtue of delegated faculties, he can demand taxes only if this is especially permitted to him. In the New Code canon 1056 we read: Ordinaries and their officials may not de-

---

[24] Wernz, no. 636, note 180.

[25] Bargilliat, n. 414; S. Off. Feb. 22, 1899.

[26] Acta S. Sed. I ap. XIII.

[27] Gasparri, n. 324; Wernz, n. 634.

mand any emolument, when granting a dispensation, with the exception of a small offering for defraying the expenses of the Chancery in dispensations for those who are not poor, unless a faculty herefor be granted them expressly by the Holy See and if they shall have exacted anything, they are held to restitution. All customs to the contrary are hereby declared illegal.

No regard need be had to the future, provided the petitioners are poor at present. The rich relatives are not considered nor capital encumbered by debts or borrowed.[28] In no way does error or fraud as to the pecuniary position of the petitioners affect the validity of the dispensation.[29] Those who live solely by the labor of their hands are not only poor, they are considered to be destitute.[30] The canon does not forbid the acceptance of voluntary gifts, and after the dispensation has been executed it is not prohibited to accept what is freely offered.[31] For the exercution of matrimonial dispensations the Ordinary is forbidden to ask or demand voluntary remuneration. He is allowed only what the papal rescript permits him, such as chancery fees and expenses.[32]

Specimens of petitions and how they must be addressed are found in various authors as Sabetti Barrett, Noldin, De Smet, especially Capello. Ordinaries, when dispensing in virtue of delegated faculties follow the rules and prescriptions of the Curia also in this: State the faculties and for how long they enjoy these faculties; grant the dispensations in writing and rarely by telephone or telegraph. The dispensation would be valid but illicit if the faculties are not mentioned in the episcopal rescripts. The powers granted to Ordinaries contain no invalidating clause and canon 1057 merely states: Qui ex potestate a Sede Apostolica delegata dispensationem concedunt, in eadem expressam pontificii indulti mentionem faciant. The Bishops are only obliged to follow the Style of the Curia in so far as the substance of the concession is concerned, the formalities are no longer binding since the clause "*alias nullae sint*" is now omitted in the indults. The formalities must be observed for licitness but only in so far as time, place and matters permit.[33]

---

[28] Reiff. App. n. 379; Schmalzgr. IV, tit. 16 n. 131.

[29] Capello, p. 531.

[30] Wernz, n. 634; Gasparri, n. 318.

[31] Sanchez, lib. VII, disp. 35, n. 14; Reiff. App. 321.

[32] Wernz, n. 639; Gasparri, n. 430; D'Annibale, p. 111, par. 502, note, 15; Giovine, tom. II, par. 55; Reiff. App. n. 319; Schmalzgr. lib. VIII, disp. 35, n. 12.

[33] Wernz, 638; Gasparri, 454.

CHAPTER X

Concession and Execution of Dispensations

The Holy See and the Ordinaries generally grant dispensations by simple rescripts. These rescripts are sometimes given in "*forma gratiosa*," and when this is done, as for instance, dispensations for royalties or "sanatio in radice" they are applied directly to the petitioners.[1]

Ordinarily, however, dispensations are granted in "*commissarial form*," where the executor is either an executor necessarius or voluntarius. The executor necessarius exercises mere ministerial powers. He examines and verifies the facts contained in the supplica and then in full conformity with the rescript, imposes the penance, absolves, dispenses and legitimates the children.[2] He cannot refuse to execute the dispensation unless the rescript is manifestly vitiated by subreption or obreption, or the executor is certain that the conditions placed in the grant have not been fulfilled, or the petitioner is so unworthy that the granting of the favor would cause scandal, but in this latter case the Holy See would have to be notified, why the dispensation has been refused.[3]

Dispensations granted without an executor go into effect immediately and hence the causes must be true, when the dispensation is granted. When the agency of an executor is employed, the dispensation is not in force until the time of the execution and it suffices if the causes of the petition be present at that time.[4]

The delegated faculties which our Ordinaries enjoy are granted in the commissarial form, but the Ordinaries are "executores voluntarii." They may therefore grant the dispensations either in full, with certain restrictions, or refuse them altogether.[5]

Both the executor necessarius and the executor voluntarius may prudently employ a substitute unless the rescript expressly states otherwise. They are always permitted to delegate an-

---

[1] Wernz, n. 638; Putzer, p. 97.

[2] Reiff. App. n. 291; Wernz, n. 638.

[3] Canon 54; Normae pec. cap. III, nos. 3 and 4; De Smet, p. 226.

[4] Canons 38, 39; Reiff. App. n. 220; Schmalzgr. lib. IV, tit. 16, n. 160.

[5] Normae pec cap. III, nos. 3 and 4; Capello, p. 523.

other to verify the facts of the petition.[6] No executor can validly exercise his office before he has received the rescript, unless the notice bears the official approbation.[7] Important decrees on this matter were issued by the S. C. S. O. (24 Aug., 1892) and the S. Penitentiaria (15 Jan., 1894) stating: "that the dispensation cannot be executed on notice by telegram, that the dispensation has been granted unless the telegram was officially sent by the Holy See."[8] The S. Penitentiaria sends its rescripts either to the Ordinary or to the priest, indicating the method of execution. The dispensation is granted either in the extra-sacramental forum as the one mentioned in the chapter "Dumodo sit occultum," or in the sacramental forum by the confessor, but always in the forum of conscience, never in the external forum. When the sacramental forum is in question, the rescript goes directly to the confessor unopened, whether the petition was sent by the confessor directly to the Holy See or whether it was forwarded to Rome through the episcopal Chancery Office. The confessor cannot subdelegate his powers when the letters determine the confessor. When the petitioner himself has applied, the rescript generally reads: "Discreto viro Confessario ex probatis ab Ordinario per latorem praesentium eligendo." The petitioner is then free to choose the confessor and also to select another, when the priest first chosen is dead or is hindered by sickness or other causes, or is inexperienced, or too strict, or even if the confessor has declared the letters subreptitious or obreptitious. The confessor must always be from among those approved by the Ordinary of the place.[9]

EPISCOPAL DISPENSATIONS

The confessor before applying to the Bishop for a dispensation, will ask himself: is the impediment or the case occult in the sense pointed out? Is there a sufficient cause? Can a dispensation be granted in the case? Dispensations can be asked for orally, but it is not at all expedient. The case must be investigated, the petition examined, and when the rescript is given, clauses must be inserted and all this cannot be properly done orally. Furthermore, the impediment, when it is proposed orally,

---

[6] Can. 57; Reiff. n. 325; Sanchez, VIII, disp. 35; Schmalzgr. IV, t. 16, n. 226.

[7] Canon 53.

[8] Reiff. App. n. 299; Schmalzgr. IV, t. 16, n. 222; Wernz, n. 618, note 80.

[9] Feije, De imped. n. 748; Ferreres, La Curia n. 873; Gasparri, n. 411, 432; Sanchez, lib. VIII, D. 27, n. 40; Reiffenstuel, App. n. 451.

is often not well expressed, and when the dispensation is granted, things are easily omitted that may render the dispensation void. Hence the Bishop generally will demand that the supplica be drawn up and contain, in substance at least, all that is essential according to the Style of the Curia and as we have pointed out. The confessor of course must avoid the mention of anything by which the petitioner could be identified.[10] The episcopal dispensations are executed in the same way as the dispensations granted by the Holy See. The executor is either the Bishop himself, the parish priest or the confessor. Generally episcopal dispensations are granted in gracious form and hence the Bishop carries out the execution himself. The parish priest for the extra-sacramental forum, and the confessor for the sacramental forum, will therefore have nothing else to do but to communicate to the parties, that absolution, dispensation, legitimation have been granted and impose upon the petitioner what is prescribed by the Bishop. To dispense in gracious form is the better way, though the conditions must be verified, when the dispensation is granted and not, when it is communicated to the parties by the priest or confessor. If the causes are true, when the Bishop grants the dispensation it is valid, even though the causes and conditions have changed by the time it is communicated.[11]

When the Bishop dispenses by delegated powers, the rescript makes mention of the apostolic authority and the text of the indult; then follows the absolution ad effectum, the juridical absolution if necessary, penance, clauses, dispensation and legitimation. It would not suffice for instance to say: the petitioners are free to marry.[12] If the faculties are not mentioned the dispensation is valid but illicit. This opinion of D'Annibale[13] is confirmed by a response of the S. C. Inq. (15 June, 1875), Sabetti-Baarrett[14] and the new Code (can. 1057).

When the Ordinary dispenses from two impediments, he follows the method indicated, namely, he dispenses from the public first and then by a separate rescript from the occult, revalidating at the same time the dispensation granted from the external forum.[15]

---

[10] Reiff. App. n. 490; Sanchez, lib. III, D. 31, lib. VIII, D. 29.

[11] Reiff. App. 206; Sanchez, lib. VIII, D. 24.

[12] Giovini, p. 1, par. 89; Noldin, n. 638; D'Ann. p. 111, par. 503, note 16.

[13] D'Annibale, p. 111, par. 503, note 18.

[14] Sabetti-Barrett, n. 926.

[15] Statuta Synod. dioces. Balt. an. 1886, pp. 108-109; Wernz, 633; Gasparri, no. 326; Putzer, n. 86.

When the parish priest or confessor has communicated the dispensation in the extra-sacramental forum, the document is placed in the secret archives, and the dispensation is recorded in the special register for occult cases. The confessor, who dispenses in the sacramental forum communicates the dispensation and then destroys the rescript because it can serve no other purpose.

When the priest dispenses in virtue of delegated faculties he is the executor voluntarius and hence he may grant the dispensation or refuse it. In conformity with canon 54, prudence and conscience should be his guides in the exercise of these powers, and unless he fulfills the essential conditions of the rescript and observes the substantial form of procedure, the dispensations are null and void (can. 55).

In examining the conditions it is sufficient "for the delegated judge to satisfy his conscience, as to the truth of the facts.[16] It depends therefore on the prudent judgment of the delegate, regard being had to the particular circumstances of each case, which might make it necessary or desirable to interrogate the parties as well as the witnesses.[17]

INTERPRETATION OF CLAUSES

In the execution of matrimonial dispensations, special attention must be paid to the clauses, which are contained in the rescripts. Some clauses are prescriptive and must be observed under pain of nullity, others are more directive, which when not heeded, render the execution illicit only. Since the decree of the S. C. S. O. (Aug. 28, 1885), the clauses have been reduced and changed considerably.[18] It was difficult at times to distinguish between directive and prescriptive clauses, to judge which must be observed for validity and which for licetness.

The New Code has simplified matters also in this matter. In all rescripts only those conditions are essential and required for validity, which are mentioned with the particles, "si, dummodo," or an equivalent term (can. 38). The clause "*si preces veritate nitantur*" when not expressed is always to be understood (can. 40). The two exceptions to this rule, have reference to dispensations granted by a Motu proprio (can. 45) or dispensations from minor impediments (1054) and have been explained before.

---

[16] S. Penitentiaria July 1, 1859.

[17] S. Penitentiaria Sep. 5, 1899; Cf. Rth. fr. 1900, p. 88; De Smet, n. 390.

[18] Wernz, n. 640.

The clauses: "si vera sint exposita, si ita est, si preces veritate nitantur," formerly read: "si per informationem eandem preces veritate niti repereris."[19] In the future the objective truth is alone considered for the validity of the rescript, and the clause therefore; "de praemissis te diligenter informes" is only required for the licit execution of dispensations. If the executor knows that the impediment, causes, circumstances are as they were written down, he can immediately proceed to the execution of the rescript.

"Discreto viro confessario ex probatis ab Ordinario loci per latorem eligendo." A confessor from another diocese is not eligible nor can one approved for men only, hear the women.[20]

"Discreto viro N Confessario." This clause determines the confessor and is inserted, when the petitioner mentioned the confessor or when the confessor has applied for the penitent. When the confessor opens the letter and does not wish to accept or does not execute the dispensation for reasons of his own, the petitioner can choose another. It suffices for validity to execute the dispensation for one, when grave reasons demand it.[21] The confessor must inquire and verify the facts in confession. He believes what the penitent tells him unless he knows outside of confession that the dispensation is vitiated by false statements.[22] If the confessor has executed the dispensation without verifying the facts, the dispensation is valid, providing the necessary requirements are objectively present.[23]

If the rescript contains the words: "*in foro conscientiae,*" sacramental confession is not necessary. When the sacramental confession is mentioned the dispensation can only be granted in confession. A sacrilegious confession does not render the dispensation invalid. If the confessor sees that the penitent is not well disposed, he should try to render him worthy. If it is impossible, it is well to postpone the execution of the rescript, unless it is a case of urgent necessity, when the dispensation can be granted.[24] Dispensation can be granted before the absolution

[19] S. C. S. O. Aug. 28, 1885; S. Penitent. Apr. 27, 1886; Gasparri, n. 397; Wernz, n. 640, note 209.

[20] Benedict XIV, Inst. eccl. 87, n. 31; D'Annibale, I, 242-245.

[21] Feije, De Imp. n. 758; De Smet, n. 397.

[22] Schmalzg. lib. IV, tit. XVI, n. 224; Sanchez, lib. VIII, D. 35; Reiff. App. n. 324.

[23] Sanchez, lib. VIII, D. 34, n. 25; Wernz, n. 640; Gasparri, n. 397.

[24] Apud. Carriere, De Matr. n. 1168. S. Penit.; Reiff. App. n. 457; Sanchez, VIII, D. 34, n. 29.

even when the absolution must be deferred.[25] In executing the rescript care should be taken to dispose the penitent for absolution from sin, but the absolution ad effectum is valid, provided the confession took place.[26]

"*Prolem susceptam, si qua sit, legitimam decernendo.*" If legitimation has been forgotten, it can be made afterwards and the child would be considered legitimate, from the time that the dispensation was granted. Legitimation can take place even after the death of the parents, even when the death occurred before the marriage took place, provided the dispensation had been granted, or even when death prevented the execution of the rescript.[27]

"*Praesentibus laniatis.*" To escape penalty it would suffice to break the seal and tear the rescript, because they could then no longer be used in court, but the clause must be observed, especially when it contains the words "*per te combustis.*" The rescript should be destroyed within three days, but it may be kept until after the marriage. If the confessor gives the rescript to the petitioner, the dispensation would be valid, but the rescript has no judicial value unless the confessor has refused to execute the rescript.[28] The confessor acts in the external forum as though he knew nothing.[29] Documents for the sacramental forum, can never be alleged as proofs for the external forum. The S. Penitentiaria demans this to safeguard the secrecy of the confessional. Unavoidable and distressing consequences sometimes arise from this discipline. Sometimes marriages which are lawful in the internal forum must be considered invalid in the external forum. Presumptions for validity might be lawful for the internal forum and prove nothing before a matrimonial court. The judge is not concerned with the internal forum. When he declares the marriage invalid, his sentence does not militate against the internal forum or the natural law, provided the laws of the external forum have been observed.[30] The conflict between both forums cannot be avoided entirely. Many difficulties have been eliminated by the abrogation of some impediments and

---

[25] S. Peniten. Episcopo Tudelensi May 19, 1834; Jan. 4, 1839; Gasparri 412.

[26] Lega, De Judiciis p. 339, n. 277.

[27] Wernz, n. 640; Gasparri, n. 403; Sanchez, lib. VIII, D. 2; D. 34 n. 43.

[28] Reiff. App. n. 482; Schmalzgr. lib. IV, tit. 16, n. 252.

[29] Reiff. App. n. 481.

[30] Scherer, p. 453, note 2; Benedict XIV, Inst. eccl. 87, n. 49; Wernz, n. 609, note 10; Gasparri, n. 472; Sanchez, lib. III, D. 15; Reiff. App. n. 480 sq.

other changes made by the New Code. In many cases the conflict is prevented by the S. Penitentiaria. It grants rescripts for the extra-sacramental forum with the admonition to keep a record of the dispensation in the secret archives. Thus, when a marriage is null on account of the impediment of clandestinity and the parties are considered lawful man and wife, the S. Penitentiaria in granting dispensation does not insert the words *laniatis* or *conbustis*. When no record is made of the dispensation, the sworn testimony of the husband or wife, claiming the validity of the marriage is sometimes admitted as sufficient proof in the external forum.[31]

The foregoing clauses must be strictly observed for validity. Other clauses point out obligations of the natural law e. g. avoiding scandal and the occasion of sin, or of the positive law such as publication of the banns. These are merely admonitions, which must be followed under pain of sin, but do not render the dispensation invalid.[32] The clauses containing demands for penance or alms are prescriptive for the external forum but only of an earnest appeal in the internal forum.[33]

The dispensation cannot be licitly given unless the promise is made to remove the scandal and as far as possible the occasion of sin. The separation of the parties cannot be imposed, when it is not expedient, but reparation must be made according to the advice of the executor.[34]

"*Imposita eis . . . gravi poenitentia.*" The dispensation is valid but illicit if penance is not imposed.[35] "In determining the quality, gravity, duration, etc., of the penance, which according to law is left to the discretion of the delegate, he must not be either too severe or too indulgent, and he must take into account the condition, age, weakness, employment, sex, etc., of those upon whom he is enjoined to impose it."[36]

"*Et aliis quae de iure fuerit iniungenda.*" Restoration and reparation must be made and, besides the juridical penance, the sacramental penance must not be omitted. Some clauses are easily understood and need not be mentioned here, others have been abrogated and are no longer in use.[37]

---

[31] Cf. Instr. Card. R. par. 170 sq.; Cap. 7, X de frig. IV, 15; Wernz, n. 745.

[32] Wernz, n. 640.

[33] Wernz, n. 640; Zitelli, p. 98; Putzer, p. 85.

[34] S. Peniten. 12 Apr., 1889; Gasparri, n. 401; 424; S. Penitent. 27 Apr., 1886.

[35] Sanchez, lib. VIII D. 34. n. 29; Reiff. App. n. 341.

[36] S. Penitent. 25 Feb., 1890.

[37] Gasparri, n. 396 sq. Wernz, n. 640. note 209 sq.

One clause deserves special mention: "Et quod oratores . . . a quibusvis ecclesiasticis sententiis, censuris et poenis . . . ad effectum huius dispensationis dumtaxat . . . absolvantur." The absolution is only granted to remove the obstacle to the lawful execution of the dispensation but leaves the censure unaffected otherwise. It is of practical importance for instance for the revalidation of a marriage contracted before a Protestant minister.[38] The excommunicated could formerly receive no rescripts.[39]

The clause was modified by Pius X[40] who excluded only the excommunicated by name and those suspended a divinis by the Holy See. The New Code has made another change in the matter. Canon 36, 2, partly taken from Normae peculiares (cap. 3, n. 6) reads: "Favors and dispensations of every kind granted by the Holy See are valid even for those under censure, except for such as are excommunicated (can. 2265, 2), interdicted (can. 2275, n. 3) and suspended (can. 2283) by a declaratory or condemnatory sentence." The absolution ad effectum is therefore no longer necessary for the valid execution of a dispensation, except when there is question of these three censures. For the validity of the absolution from these three it is necessary that they receive special mention in the papal rescript (can. 2265, 2).

The absolution ad effectum is always required for the licit use of the rescript. Formerly the opinions differed on this point.[41] The Church does not wish to grant favors to the unworthy, but she willingly extends her help to those who seek it. All those, who have faculties to dispense, enjoy the additional powers, which are necessary for the exercise of those faculties. The powers therefore to absolve from ecclesiastical penalties, that the dispensation may take effect, is always included in the faculties of dispensing (can. 66).

The foregoing clause must not be confounded with another in virtue of which the executor can absolve from censure not merely to make the dispensation effective but so that the censure will not revive. This absolution removes the censure and faults for the external and consequently before both forums or before the internal forum alone according as it is given for the external or the internal forum.[42]

---

[38] Reiff. App. n. 310; Wernz, n. 640, note 214.

[39] S. C. de P. F. 26 Sep., 1821; S. C. Inq. 18 Dec., 1872; Wernz, n. 640, note 214.

[40] Normae pecul. 29 Sep., 1908. c. 3. n. 6; Capello, page 525.

[41] De Smet, n. 393 p. 321; Ferreres, La Curia 235-237.

[42] Reiff. App. n. 343; De Smet, n. 241.

The final act of execution of the dispensation is called fulmination of the rescript. When the facts have been sufficiently verified, the conditions fulfilled, the clauses observed, the decree of *execution* is issued. In this the executor for the extra-sacramental forum absolves from censures, imposes the penance, gives advice, how scandal is to be removed and finally dispenses and legitimates the offspring.[43] No such decree is required for the valid *fulmination* or communication of the dispensation. It may be made orally or by telegram not only validly but licitly also in case of necessity, but ordinarily a written document must be drawn up so as to furnish proof for the external forum. The document of execution with the evidence of fulmination must be preserved in the secret archives of the Curia and the parish priest makes a note of it in the secret marriage register to be able to show in case of necessity that the dispensation has been granted.

In the sacramental forum, the confessor chosen by the petitioners or determined by the S. Penitentiaria or the Ordinary receives the sealed rescript and proceeds to verify the facts, observes the conditions and clauses and then by an express or tacit consent of the petitioners executes and fulminates the dispensation. All this is done in sacramental confession, by word of mouth. The order to be followed is given in the formula employed in the curia and is contained in the Ritual.[44] The S. Penitentiaria however demands no special formula and it suffices for validity to determine the nature of the impediment and give the dispensation.[45] Dispensation is granted to the one bound by the impediment or the guilty party. When the impediment is common to both, as adultery with the promise of marriage, the rescript is executed in respect to both.[46] When it is impossible or very difficult to induce the other party to go to confession, it suffices for validity to dispense one.[47]

It is necessary to mention the change in the old discipline with regard to the renewal of consent. When a marriage is invalid on account of an occult impediment it suffices for the convalidation, that the one who knows of the impediment renew the consent, provided the other has not retracted the consent. If both parties are aware of the invalidity both must renew their consent, but it may be done privately and secretly, either in confession or outside of confession (can. 1135, 2, 3).

[43] S. Penitentiaria 27 Apr., 1886; Gasparri, n. 424.
[44] Putzer, p. 95; Gasparri, n. 431; De Smet, n. 397.
[45] Capello, p. 361; Bargilliat, n. 486; Noldin, n. 639.
[46] S. Penitent. 15 Nov., 1748.
[47] Feije, n. 758.

When the petitioners refuse the dispensation, it cannot be granted, but the rescript can be retained for future use.[48] In a response of the S. Penitentiaria we read: "The faculty remains even after the destruction of the letters, but the letters may be kept as long as there is any probability that the penitent will appear, care being taken to avoid the danger of losing them.[49] Even if one of the petitioners married, the dispensation could be granted after the death of the partner.[50]

ERRORS IN THE RESCRIPT AND HOW TO REMEDY THEM

An essential error in the rescript invalidates the dispensation (can. 55). Obreption and subreption in one part of the rescript do not affect the other part, when the rescript contains more than one favor (can. 42).

1. Exaggeration does not vitiate the dispensation, if the final cause in itself is true,[51] but when this is false and the rescript is granted for a major impediment, the dispensation is void. 2. When the final cause, for which the dispensation was granted has ceased, e. g., the child to be legitimated died, we must distinguish: If the child died after the dispensation had been executed, the impediment once removed does not revive, even though the child died before the marriage was contracted. If the child died before the rescript for the major impediment was executed, the dispensation is invalid.[52] When the marriage is contracted and the parties are ignorant of the fact that a substantial error invalidated the dispensation, they can be left in good faith in most cases.[53] Many authors defend the opinion that an error discovered after the marriage ceremony, even in regard to the final cause, does not invalidate the marriage.[54]

HOW TO REMEDY DEFECTIVE RESCRIPTS

If the execution of an apostolic or episcopal dispensation has been vitiated by neglecting an essential element, the executor can begin to execute the dispensation again without a fresh dis-

---

[48] Sanchez, lib. VIII. D. 32. n. 6; Wernz, n. 641; Gasparri, n. 428; Ojetti, Syn. n. 1824; De Smet, n. 392.

[49] Lintzer Quartalschrift 1905. p. 582; Noldin, 1. n. 172; De Smet, n. 397.

[50] Gasparri, n. 429; Sanchez, lib. VIII. D. 32 n. 6; D'Annibale, p. 111, par. 364 note 30.

[51] Sanchez, lib. VIII. D. 21; Reiff. App. n. 205.

[52] Can. 86; Reiff. App. 227.

[53] Gasparri, n. 390.

[54] Schmalzgr. lib. IV. t. 16. n. 166; Sanchez, Lib. VIII. D. 17. n. 8; De Smet, n. 403.

pensation, unless his power has expired on account of cessation of the final cause or the rescript has been recalled.[55] When the executor cannot correct the mistake, he must procure letters known as "*perinde valere,*" in virtue of which a favor previously granted is revalidated so that by a fiction of the law, the effect of the revalidation is regarded as going back to the time of the original granting of the dispensation.[56] In asking for these letters, the petitioner will apply the same rules that obtained in writing for the first rescript, adding the causes, errors and defects, which rendered the first dispensation void.[57] Should it happen that another error has been committed, a new letter called "*perinde valere super perinde valere*" would be required.

If the first dispensation was for a public impediment and the fresh impediment is an occult one, "*perinde valere*" will be granted for the internal forum and mention must be made of the public impediment. When dispensation has been granted from two impediments, one occult the other public and the new impediment is occult, all three impediments are mentioned and the dispensation is revalidated in the internal forum. When the new impediment is public, it is removed in the external forum and then the dispensation is revalidated in the forum of conscience.

In virtue of delegated faculties, the Ordinaries possess various powers for revalidating dispensation. By ordinary powers they can remedy defective dispensation from Rome, when they are invalid on account of some occult defect in case of urgent necessity. The priest and confessor can only revalidate dispensations for which they have faculties i. e. in cases of urgent necessity and in danger of death, unless they have special powers for dispensations.

This brings us to the end of our task. The New Code with its many changes, has made a study of the S. Penitentiaria and its relations to faculties of Ordinaries and priests, very opportune. Since Ordinaries and priests enjoy many faculties, which were formerly reserved to this S. Tribunal, it is well to know and imitate its mode of procedure in the internal forum. To the praise of the S. Penitentiaria be it said that everything is performed and expedited with the profoundest secrecy and free of any charges.

---

[55] Can. 59; Sanchez, L. VIII. D. 27. n. 39; Schmalzgr., L. I. t. n. 40; Wernz, n. 641; Gasparri, n. 429; D'Annibale, p. I. par. 77. n. 55; De Smet, n. 405 sq.

[56] Gasparri, n. 390; Giovini, tom. II. par. 82. n. 4 sq.; Wernz, n. 642; De Smet, n. 405; Reiff. App. n. 362.

[57] Putzer, p. 95; De Smet, 405 sq.

Its officials take an oath to this effect: "Ego N ab hac hora in antea ero fidelis et oboediens B. Petro et Domino Nostro Papae, eiusque successoribus canonice intrantibus; Officium meum fideliter exercebo, et gratis; eiusque ratione, nihil ab aliquibus, etiam sponte oblatum, vel donatum, accipiam, praeter quam salarium, mihi constitutum; secreta S. Poenitentiariae et occultos casus ac personas, de quibus in ea tractabitur, nunquam cuiquam, extra Officium revelabo; et ita iuro ad Sacrosancta Dei Evangelia." Every official, when he assumes the office, takes this oath before the Chief Penitentiary and it is repeated every year in the first meeting of the Signatura. The penalty for violating the oath is most severe. "Any one, who contrary to the oath, accepts even the smallest gift from the petitioners, be it for more prompt expedition or extraordinary labor in procuring, writing, reviewing or examining the rescript, or under any plea or pretence, is ipso facto deprived of his office and punished with excommunication from which no one outside of danger of death, can absolve, but the Roman Pontiff." Furthermore any one convicted of this crime, becomes infamous and is incapable of receiving future offices. Officials who by fraud or trickery suggest to others how petitions may be more easily obtained, incur the same punishment (Benedict XIV "In Apostolicae," 13 Apr., 1744). These penalties are not abrogated by the New Code. According to canon 243 the Congregations, Tribunals and Offices of the Roman Curia are governed by the disciplinary laws and regulations defined and determined for each organization.

Who does not see that when all rules are observed, the S. Penitentiaria is a tribunal of mercy, instituted for the welfare of souls, as Benedict XIV has said? For this reason the seal of the S. Tribunal appropriately bears the image of the Virgin Mother with the Holy Infant in her arms. God promised mercy and grace to penitents and our Holy Mother the Church follows His example in dispensing His gifts. "The bruised reed He shall not break and the smoking flax He shall not quench. He shall bring forth judgment unto truth" (Is. 42, 3).

APPENDIX

PART I

Taxes

The so-called Tax-lists constitute an important chapter in the history of the Sacred Penitentiaria. The great controversy between Catholics and non-Catholics concerning Tax-lists cover many pages of historical research and, if we are to judge by the bitter remarks found in books and magazines, the time has not yet come for an unbiased solution.

There is nothing good or sacred in this world, that has not been abused by men. We are therefore not astonished to find abuses in the Church. The Church, of divine institution, but existing amongst men, is exposed to their imperfections and frailties. The one important task for us is not so much to give minute details of these abuses, but rather to show that the Church of Christ as such, has never approved but always condemned these abuses. To her glory be it said, that she never had an agreement with vice. Simony has been combated by the Church since the time of Simon Magus, its first perpetrator.

The great struggle of Gregory VII in the matter of investiture, during the time when German Emperors created bishops and antipopes and committed depredations throughout Germany and Italy, is a classical example of the battle of the Church against simony. To be sure churchmen, protected by civil power, have at times, under pretence of indigence or instigated by greed and malice, tried to sell spiritual goods for temporal gain, but the Church, as a social and ecclesiastical body, has ever disowned them and condemned their practices.

Concessions and grants of spiritual favors by the Sacred Penitentiaria require the payment of certain taxes. These are not the price for favors, as we shall endeavor to prove, but originally merely meant to make up the salary of the officials employed. No doubt there is an element of danger in the transaction but such danger, common to all institutions, secular as well as ecclesiastical, is parried by laws and repression of abuses.

It is difficult to fix the time when the Sacred Penitentiaria issued the first tax-list. Such lists may have been in existence, when Thomas of Capua composed his Formulary, since Benedict XII in his Constitution presupposes them.[1] In this same constitution the Pope demands, that the petitions must all be returned to the senders, and this is one of the reasons why our sources are so fragmentary.[2] The tax-list published with this Constitution "In agro dominico," is one of the oldest documents we have.[3] In the introduction the object and the legitimate reasons for imposing taxes are clearly pointed out. "Ut igitur scriptores Sacrae Poenitentiariae domini papae in recipiendo pro scriptura litterarum de Poenitentiariae litteris procurandis de cetero non excedant, infrascriptas taxationes . . . faciendas duximus et praesentibus annotandas." This regulation, published for the first time by H. Denifle, was official and almost all formulas of concessions are represented in this list. It is the belief of some authors, that this list is based on a still older document and it cannot be denied that taxes may have been in use before, but this is the earliest extant official document on the subject.

When did the Sacred Penitentiariea begin to levy taxes? This is a difficult question to answer, since we have no record in history. We may say that they were imposed before the time of Benedict XII, because we find taxes mentioned in a few letters prior to that Pope, but they are very rare, because as we have stated, the petitions were returned to the senders. Even up to the time of Clement V (d. 1314) no regular record of the honoraria was kept. A list of taxes is contained in a document dated July 14, 1311. The custom of imposing taxes seems to be well established after July, 1320. At this time taxes were always mentioned, with the species of money abbreviated and the names of the distributors. In the year 1336, we find the Florin (about $2.42½) and towards the close of the year 1342 the Turonensis Grossus (about 17¾c) is given. It is of interest to note the precaution taken against abuses by placing the tax between two parts of the name of the petitioner as for instance, W. de Argenquatuor tur-tina (W. de Argentina quatuor tur).

To prove that the taxes were not a price for favors granted, but the salary of the officials, we need only give a cursory glance

---

[1] Vat. Archivum Armarium 53 no. 17, ff 10 v-12 v. Denifle. Archiv fur Litt. u. Kirch. vol. IV pp. 237-238.

[2] Armarium 53 no. 17 ff 26-35.

[3] Denifle, Die aelteste Taxrolle der ap. Poenitent. Archiv. f. Litt. u. Kirch. des Mittelalters. vol. IV, 1888, pp. 201 sq. Taxes of the Papal Penitentiary, English Historical Review, vol. VIII, 1893, p. 424.

over the original documents. Among the many, we find the list of taxes of the Grand Penitentiary Gaucelme de Jean (1338). We read there "*taxationes pro littera*," which means a payment for the scribe for composing the letter. The formula which is most frequently met with is: "Turonensis pro littera confessionali in minori forma," another "littera confessionali in maiori forma duo turonenses." For annonymous or for particular letters the taxes were from three to six tur., and one "absolutio et dispensatio de omnibus sententiis generalibus et aliis multis casibus," demands seven tur. The amount of taxes was rated according to the length of the letter, and the more words required for the dispensation the higher were the taxes. Favors, absolutions and dispensations granted to a large number of persons, required a correspondingly higher tax. Thus we find one formula of 70 tur., 5½ florins, "pro littera generalis absolutionis in multis casibus et dispensatione pro toto ordine Cluniacensi."

We conclude that the difference in taxes is of little or no importance. It depends solely on the length of the letter, the form of the rescript and the number of the petitioners. Greatness of the favor or the gravity of the crime, does not enter into consideration. "Littera pro dispensatione super defectu natalium" requires the same amount of taxes as the dispensation for the murder of a cleric, four turonenses grossi. Protestant editions of the tax-lists also show, how little relation the taxes bear to the sin remitted. "Pro laico a lapsu carnis super quocumque actu libidinoso in foro conscientiae, tur. 6 ducat. 2; ab incestu pro laico in foro conscientiae tantum tur. 4; ab adulterio cum incestu, pro una persona tantum tur. sex."[4]

The Constitution of Benedict XII provides for cases not mentioned in the tax-list. "Quod si quando aliquae formae huismodi litterarum apparent, quae sub dictis taxationibus minime includuntur, super earum taxationibus, si commode fieri poterit, dominus noster Summus Pontifex consulatur et quod interim secundum beneplacitum Maioris Poenitentiarii taxentur."

It is necessary to bear in mind, that the same favors granted by the Penitentiaria require a higher tax if accorded by the Chancery. The Chancery has a more complicated practice of expediting matters and therefore demands higher taxes.[5] The Penitentiaria, according to the regulations of Benedict XII, de-

[4] Taxe de Parties casuelles de la Boutique du Pape, Anec. Annotationes &c. A. D. C. Antoine du Pinet A. Lyon 1564, pp. 81-82.

Denifle 1888 Archiv. fur Litt u. Kirch. des Mitt. Band IV. p. 201.

[5] Mittheilungen des Instituts fur oesterreich. Gescrichtsforschung Band. XIII, 1.

mands no more than 4½ tur. unless the rescripts apply to many and require changes, in which cases 20, 40 or even 70 tur. are asked. The scribes were not the only officials to work on these letters. Procurators prepared the petitions, "supplices libellas," and were therefore entitled to a remuneration for their work. The Pope and the Curia made no special provisions concerning the fees for the labor of procurators. According to the general regulations of the Curia, the procurators were forbidden to receive more than ½ tur. "pro littera confessionali," 2 "pro littera communi," 3, "pro completa facti narratione," 6, "pro littera declaratoria."[6] The scribe had to pay for the wax since the "sigillator nihil omnino recipiat a quocumque, nisi dumtaxat a scriptoribus dicti officii, a quibus pro cera non recipiat ultra 12 tur. pro singulis centenariis litterarum vel nisi ad instantiam partis (adversae) petentis fiat sigillum cum cera rubea impressa in alba pro qua non recipiat pro suo labore nisi unum turonensem." For minor offices, writing letters or sealing them, the officials received nothing, or at the most an insignificant reward. The total tax imposed constituted withal a small salary of the officials.

The laws of Benedict XII, regarding the taxes of the Sacred Penitentiaria, were for many years, strictly and conscientiously observed. Gradually abuses began to manifest themselves. Various abuses appeared within the sphere of the officials, which however, had no direct or important effect on the public at large. The distributors, actuated by greed and mercenary motives, passed over the letters of minor importance, and reserved to themselves, the petitions which brought higher taxes.

The commission of reform, instituted by the Council of Constance, had no fault to find with the taxes, but merely demanded that the officials be punished for the abuses. It likewise decreed that a copy of the taxes be affixed in a conspicuous place in the office of the Sacred Penitentiaria.

Other flagrant abuses directly affecting the people, were opposed and condemned without mercy.[7] Offices were at times

[6] "Videlicet pro qualibet littera confessionali in maiori seu in minori forma, non licet sibi recipere ultra dimidium tur. argenti, pro qualibet littera grossa et communi, utpote cum brevi et succincta narratione non ultra 2 tur. completa vero facti narratione non ultra 3 tur. pro qualibet vero littera declaratoria non ultra 6 tur."

[7] "In foro conscientiae, quod horendius est quam simoniacae pravitatis vitium; ubi non in remedium animarum sed sub colore appretiandarum chartarum crimina delinquentium aut gratiae dispensationum, praecise secundum qualitatem suam ut res profane taxantur, abusiones manifeste nefandas committendo. Protestatio Nationis Germanicae." Von der Herdt, Concilium Constant. IV. 1422.

sold to the highest bidder with the tacit consent of authority. Dietrich of Niem an official of the Chancery under Boniface IX (d. 1404), says of this Pope: "Necnon etiam suae Poenitentiariae ac Apostolicarum litterarum scriptoriae officia pacto pecuniario intercedente vendidit."

The abuses prevalent at this time have been somewhat exaggerated. The program of 1423 reduced the taxes for "*litterae absoluteriae*" only for the time of Lent. Had they been so excessive, they would no doubt have abolished them altogether. Dietrich of Niem is furthermore not an impartial witness. He is accused by Raynoldus of being bitter and unjust, "acerbus et iniquus" and of having written many gossipy pages, lacking in appreciation of difficulties and environments. But that there were some flagrant abuses can be seen by the reform movements of some of the Popes. To counteract the schemes of increasing the revenues of the Sacred Penitentiaria, Eugene IV (d. 1447) permited a new tax for the registration of a certain class of letters. The new tax consisted of a grossus papalis for "sententiis generalibus." For letters under formularies "Si inveneris" and Licet non credat" the tax was 2 grossi and for "litteris declaratoriis" 3 grossi papales.

Under Pius II (d. 1464) Nicolas of Cusa, imbued with the spirit of reform, demanded the removal of the scribes from office, if they accepted more than the law allowed them. Sixtus IV (1484) imposed stricter ordinances on procurators to remedy the abuses of excessive taxes, and certain documents indicate that a new tariff was issued to keep the scribes in check. All these laudable efforts proved vain on account of the venality of officials, and again every successful bidder, to increase his revenues, demanded higher taxes. Innocent VII (1492) tried more drastic measures than had yet been employed. He ruled that delinquents incur excommunication reserved to the Pope, that they be deprived of their emoluments, lose their offices and become ineligible to all offices of the Curia.

These drastic punishments however failed to bring about lasting reforms. New complaints were made to Alexander VI (d. 1503) because scribes and procurators showed no regard for the poor and refused to grant letters gratuitously.

Julius II (d. 1513) proved as vigorous in this regard as he had shown himself in his Bull on simony. In the Fifth Lateran Council he introduced new rules and regulations against the employees, who exceeded their faculties in regard to salaries and taxes.[8] Leo X (d. 1521) likewise made great endeavors to remedy existing abuses.

Manuscripts of this period show interesting features in the total amounts and the applications of the taxes.[9] One of the MSS. mentions a tax levied to benefit the procurators and to pay for the wax used. In consequence of this new tariff, the charges for preparing the petitions and expediting the letters surpassed the taxes, which formerly constituted the salary of the scribes.

Another important change appeared at this time in the forms themselves. Benedict XII always placed the words "*pro littera*" before the tax, which indicated, that the money was to be a salary for the officials. Later catalogues suppressed these words. We find for instances: "absolutio pro monaco qui praelatum indignum elegit, venit ad grossos septem." This is a regrettable change, since it would appear that the money no longer constituted a mere salary but a payment for the dispensation or absolution, which gives the canonist some difficulty in answering accusations.

In defence of the Church it could be rightly stated that the taxes imposed are simply a just penance for the transgression of the law, or that the constant practice of the Church in the past shows that she considers the taxes a just remuneration for clerical labor and hence does not offer or need an apology. A lenient explanation of the facts however cannot be expected from men, who find an accusation of simony much more efficacious in maligning the Church.

The Constitution "Pastoralis officii" (Dec. 13, 1513) of Leo X, and the new tax-list by the same Pope, are another praiseworthy attempt to reform the Roman Tribunals, but they are rather general and lack the precision manifested by Benedict XII. Leo X strongly insists that the auditors and the correctors

[8] "Qui in taxis, salariis seu mercedibus recipiendis, facultatibus ampliandis, modum et formam in eis expressam excedunt; nova gravamina et angarias quotidie imponentes pro eorum arbitrio pecunias expetunt et exegunt, in animarum ipsorum periculum, partium detrimentum, perniciosum exemplum et scandalum plurimorum totiusque Romanae Curiae infamiam et jacturam."

[9] One MS. from the year 1480 gives the following: "Taxae dispensationum super natalium: De solutione et solita genitus in aliquo gradu consanguinitatis gr. 12½ papales. De apostasia: Pro monacho qui exivit monasterium sine licentia et ivit ad guerras vel alibi vagavit cum habitu, venit in forma, scriptor habet 4½ proc. 3½ in totum, et hoc si est praesens gr. 8. Item similimodo si dereliquit habitum et deinde vult reverti ad monasterium cum habitu. Nota quod si est praesens, potest committi uni poenitentiario et venit ad gr. 12½."

abide by the old order of taxes, as modified by him, and rejects all regulations not directly approved by the Chief Penitentiary.[10] He also admonishes the procurators to be satisfied with half the tax, as pointed out in the Constitution, and not to burden the petitioners with higher taxes. They are also advised not to accept forbidden or unusual matters nor to extort more from the parties for expediting the letters than the law permits them.[11] He further request the correctors to be as lenient and moderate as possible in their demands for taxes. The Sacred Penitentiaria is urged to temper the rigor of the tariff with clemency and benignity and to treat the poor and needy with all charity.

Some of the taxes authorized by this Pope were: "Pro litteris de speciali" 6 turonenses; "pro litteris de speciali et expresso" 12 tur. When the "litterae pro absolutione" were added the tax was naturally higher. The reader will notice that here as above, the tax constituted merely the salary of the officials and had nothing to do with the quality of the favor granted. The difference in taxes arises from the diversity of letters or from the length of the formulas, or to some extent from the purpose of rendering the dispensation rarer.[12]

In summing up the different factors of the tax-list, in comparing the amounts of money, which the scribes, procurators and sealers received in proportion to the work, in finding that the quality of favors has no direct influence on the taxes, we come to the conclusion that there can be no ground for the suspicion of simony on the part of the Church. We have gathered enough material from the sources available to enable us to view the reproaches in their proper light and meet the accusations of our separated brethren in all sincerity. Individual abuses among men are to be expected and never surprise the serious student of history. Flagrant abuses are naturally more harmful, when as in our case, they are provoked and aggravated by the avidity of

---

[10] "Taxationes litterarum praeter antiquam ordinem et nostram modificationem factas, sub excommunicationis sententia non permittant, sed illas omnino retineant vel rejiciant, nisi aliud Summo Poenitentiario visum fuerit."

[11] "Unica media taxa sibi ex constitutione officii competente contententur nec partes in ullo plus gravent, nec prohibitas materias et insuetas expedire procurant, nec item a partibus plus quam pro expediendo negotio necessarium fuerit extorqueant."

[12] "Etsi tales praedictis implicitis impedimentis scienter contraxerint et consummaverint, tunc taxa augetur de duobus, occasione absolutionis illis impediendae."

For a complete list of taxes and their uses see: M. Goeller, vol. 2, pp. 146 sq.

mercenaries, who purchased offices and dignities rendered venal by those in authority.

The Church has constantly fought these abuses and perversions by grave penances and salutary laws issued by Popes and councils, and the just condemnation of the faithful helps to keep the avaricious within the proper bounds. Christ, the Good Shepherd of His flock, is ever mindful to keep alive the principle of reason and of Sacred Scripture, that spiritual favors are not objects of negotiation.

The Spirit of Truth prompted St. Peter to utter those memorable words, which show the sentiment of every true representative of Christ: "Keep thy money to thyself to perish with thee, because thou hast thought that the gift of God may be purchased with money" Acts vii, 18-25.

PART II

Componenda

Intimately connected with the taxes are the so-called componenda. They have this in common with the taxes, that money is demanded in connection with the favors granted, but the purpose of this fee is an entirely different one.[1]

Componenda may be defined as a certain sum of money (aside from the taxes) given in connection with the dispensation according to a given norm. Componenda are not a remuneration for work, but an amicable transaction for an agreed sum. In the past and even up to the present day the componenda have met with great opposition and difficulties.[2] The objections and difficulties arise from what would appear to be a financial transaction in spiritual matters.

The Church as we have seen, has always prohibited the traffic in spiritual things, but at the same time permits an amicable adjustment in matters, which do not come under this head. This has been the practice of the Church from the earliest times.

---

[1] Putzer, p. 25 104 sq. 302 sq.; Gasparri, no. 315 sq.; Giovini, L. II, p. 109 sq.; Feije, no. 690 sq.; Rosset, no. 2477; Leitner, p. 432 sq.; Scherer, p. 492; Kirchenlex. 111 p. 771 sq.; Saegmueller, Lehrb. der k. K. p. 186.

[2] Conc. Trid. spec. collect. t. 2. p. 609-615, sess. XXIV cap. 5 de ref. The Belgian bishops did not clearly distinguish between taxes and componenda. They petitioned the Vat. Counc. to have the taxes or componenda abolished, or if this could not be done to devise some means, by which those who pay more for the disp., do not receive it any easier than those who pay less or nothing.

From the eighth to the twelfth century the custom arose of substituting some lighter penance for the rigorous demands of the penitential canons. The penitential book of Egbert, Archbishop of York, declares (XIII, 11): "For him who can comply with what the Penitential prescribes, well and good; for him who cannot, we give counsel of God's mercy, instead of one day on bread and water, let him sing fifty psalms on his knee or seventy psalms without genuflecting. . . . But if he does not know the psalms and cannot fast, let him instead of one year on bread and water, give twenty-six solidi (solidus 1c.) in alms, fast till noon on one day of each week and till Vespers on another, and in three Lents bestow half of what he receives."

This practice of substituting the alms for the penance, is also sanctioned in the Irish Synod of 807 CXXIV, where it is stated that: "the fast of the second day of the week, may be redeemed by singing one psalter or by giving one denarius to a poor person." The Council of Tribur (895 can. LVI), in determining the penance for a homicide, authorizes the redemption (while traveling or at war) of the fast on Tues. Thur. or Sat. by paying a denarius or by caring for three poor persons. These redemptions were offered indiscriminately to all at the Council of Clermont (1095 can. II), suggesting the Crusades as a ranson for all penances.

The discipline of the sixteenth century admitted and demanded the componenda for the following cases: Commutation of vows, absolution from the crime of simony, absolving a cleric who was promoted with a fictitious title, dispensations for matrimonial impediments and restitutions.

Even at the time of Nicolas IV (d. 1292), the Penitentiary already enjoyed the privilege of commuting vows for a donation of money. Other forms of commutations were, making pilgrimages to well-known shrines, such as that of St. Alban's in England, or that of St. James in Compostella, Spain. The most important place for pilgrims, was of course, Rome. As early as the seventh century, during the time of Bede (674-735) the "*Visitatio ad Limina*" was regarded as a good work of great efficacy (Hist. eccl. vol. IV, 23). These long pilgrimages, entailing heavy expenses and a great loss of time, were soon commuted to a payment of money as alms, to be given to some pious work. Thus the pilgrimage to Compostella was commuted to the payment of a certain sum of money to be applied to the Patriarchial churches in Rome. These churches were in sore need in the thirteenth century, because the Popes were frequently forced to leave Rome on account of revolts and wars.[3]

During the time of Gregory XI (1370-1378) the Sacred Penitentiaria commuted the vows of visiting the Holy Sepulchre and other holy places to the payment of alms. A special collector was appointed at this time to receive the money. The alms asked were equal to the amount it would take to defray the expenses of the pilgrimage to St. Peter's and St. Paul's Churches.[4] This tradition of substituting other penances for vows continued in the fifteenth century. Eugene IV (d. 1447) writes: "Item possint vota etiam beatorum Petri et Pauli de Urbe ac sancti Jacobi in Compostella in alia opera pietatis mulieribus tantum commutare, et in commutatione voti sancti Jacobi et alterius peregrinationis. illud quod est consultum, quod detur pro medietate amore Dei arbitrio et consilio Ordinariorum sicque quod nihil ad eorum manus deveniat, et fiat deductio laboris et expensarum, quem et quas fecerunt et sustinuerunt peregrini hucusque veniendo personaliter et redeundo, ac alia medietas fabricis ecclesiarum patriarchalium Urbis assignetur." Clement VII (d. 1534) regulated the practice and fixed the amounts that could be asked. "Commutatio voti Sancti Sepulchri taxatur 12 tur., commutatio voti liminum Apostolorum Urbe 12 tur." He adds: "Nota quod in istis tribus immediate praecedentibus votorum commutationibus requiritur compositio cum Dataria Sanctissimi, quae fieri solet secundum qualitatem personarum interdum per litteras et interdum per nuncios ad arbitrium domini Datarii, sed compositio ordinaria in similibus votis est quadraginta ducatorum."[5]

The componenda offered when the vows are commuted, are justifiable on the ground that they merely constitute an agreement on the part of the faithful, to pay a certain sum of money to some pious cause, in place of the fulfillment of the obligation made by promise. They do not benefit the Pope or the other members of the Curia personally.

In like manner, the eleemosynary fine or componenda demanded in connection with matrimonial dispensations, have their legitimate uses. The Sacred Penitentiaria has not invented these componenda. She grants the dispensations, when the componenda have been made to the Chancery of Rome. During the fourteenth

---

[3] Edward of England in the fourteenth century had vowed a pilgrimage to Rome and was asked instead to found a monastery.

[4] M. Stiegler: Dispensat., Dispensationswesen u. Dispensationsrecht im Kirchenrecht. cap. 42 Geschichte der Dispensationstaxen.

[5] E. Goeller, II part 2, p. 1577.

century the Sacred Penitentiaria was obliged to give all componenda received for matrimonial dispensations to the Chamberlain or collector of the Apostolic Chancery.

These componenda constituted a fine for the faults, which as a rule give the occasion for the dispensation, or a check to restrain a too great frequency of petitions often based on undeserving grounds. The income from these componenda, with the exceptions of abuses, that could be expected, was invariably used for pious purposes.[6] To verify this we point to Pope Nicholas II (d. 1061), who by papal dispensation, legitimized the marriage of William of Normandy and Mathilda of Flanders. By way of penance they freely consented to found two monasteries at Caen. In 1063 the bishop of Venice petitioned Alexander II: "Si qua modo misericorditer conjunctam sibi illicite consanguineam retinere posset, et orationibus et jejuniis ac hereditatis et eleemosynarum se largitione redimere."[7] The favor was granted.

These fines, or penances for excesses as the ancients called them, originally were imposed only on those, who had contracted marriage against the laws of the Church.[8] The penal character of the componenda can be easily recognized by the following: "Eos qui divino timore proposito in suarum periculum animarum scienter in gradibus consanguinitatis et affinitatis constitutione canonica interdictis. . . . ipso excommunicationis sententiae ipso facto sujacere." In a catalogue of the fifteenth century we read, that those who contract matrimony in the fourth degree of affinity need not pay componenda, if the marriage has not been consummated; if it was consummated, they were obliged to pay the componenda and the tax. This same rule was followed a half a century later by Clement VII.[9] The same rule applied to marriages contracted in other forbidden degrees. When the marriage had been contracted in ignorance of the law no componenda was asked.

---

[6] Alexander V (d. 1410) and Martin V (d. 1431) used them to restore churches and to aid other charitable institutions.

[7] Patr. Lat. t. CXLVI, 1406.

[8] "Et quia dicti contrahentes concordare habent cum Camera Ap. de excessu praedicto." "Quod hi qui ignorantes contraxerunt in dicto sic contracto remanere, hi vero qui scientes, de novo contrahere possint dispensare, dum tales, qui scientes contraxerunt remittantur ad Cameram Ap. compositur cum eadem." E. Goeller I part II p. 43.

[9] Nota quod si matrimonium fuerit scienter contractum et consummatum in hujusmodi quarto, tunc materia est componenda cum Datario Sanctissimi, est regulariter duc. auri de Camera decem." E. Goeller, II part II p. 47.

At first, dispensations from impediments were granted mostly to the nobility, but soon their bad example found followers among all classes. To stem the abuses and to make it more difficult to obtain dispensations the Popes were obliged to employ strict laws and ordinances. Clement VII decreed: "Et insuper isto impedimento quocumque modo sit, vel de contrahendo vel contracto, scienter vel ignoranter, consummato vel non consummato, semper est componendum cum Datario Sanctissimi et compositio est 25 duc. auri de camera."[10] "Nota quod in secundo et tertio semper componitur cum Datario et de concordia non est certa taxa, quia secundum qualitatem personarum componitur communiter in tertio gradu, pro compositione solvantur ducati 25 (ducat about 60c.), pro nobilibus duplo videlicet 50." The second degree of consanguinity seemed to have this in common with the fourth, that no componenda was asked, when the origin of the impediments was the same and the marriage had been consummated. The document adds: "Si vero est consummatum componit cum Datario ad ducatos decem." A multiplex impediment arising from the collateral line was always treated according to the following norm: "Nota quod in isto gradu semper componitur cum Datario si sunt pauperes ad ducatos 25, si divites aut nobiles arbitraria est compositio, quia aliquando solvuntur duc 50." Dispensation from the impediment of the second degree of affinity, arising from illicit intercourse, even for contracted marriages was not granted except to the highest nobility and then only for a considerable componendum. For the dispensations of other impediments no eleemosynary fine was imposed.

The third series of componenda has reference to goods illicitly acquired and fruits illegitimately received. It has always been the practice of the Church to grant no absolution from sins against the seventh commandment, unless restitution of ill-gotten goods was assured. It was formerly the custom of the Sacred Penitentiaria to tax illegitimate profits and to demand that restitution be made and a certain sum of money be given as penance for the transgression. E. Goller in his study of the Sacred Penitentiaria, gives many examples. To mention two will suffice to show the practice of the Sacred Tribunal. One is taken from the catalogue of the taxes, issued by the Sacred Penitentiaria in the first quarter of the sixteenth century. A merchant, who transported arms and other articles to the infidels, without personal

[10] E. Goeller l. c. p. 149.

profit, was taxed six tur. In a note it is stated, that if he derived any benefit from this transaction, the matter was to be adjusted with the Dataria and the tax to be levied accordingly. The second example is similar to this. One who has derived considerable profit form goods unlawfully acquired, is obliged to pay the componenda to the Dataria.[11]

In summing up this brief treatise on taxes, we find that in the Roman Curia the expenses incurred by petitioners fall under four heads:

1. Expenses or carriage (postage, etc., also a fee to the accredited agent, when one has been employed);
2. A tax to be used in defraying the expenses incurred by the Holy See in the organized administration of dispensations;
3. The componendum to be paid to the congregations and tribunals and applied by them to pious uses;
4. An alms imposed on the petitioners and to be distributed by themselves in good works.

The first two are merely a just compensation for the expenses incurred by the Curia. The last is without reproach, since Sacred Scripture in numerous places inculcates the giving of alms.[12] Authors of the Middle Ages taught that alms were most efficacious.[13] It is also recommended and presupposed in certain parts of the Roman Ritual.[14]

As to the third point, the componenda in themselves are legitimate and can be justified as we have endeavored to prove. Wherever you turn, you will not find any cause to accuse the Church as such of simony. Her laws are without reproach. There have been grave abuses and some perhaps still exist. Officials have profited by their positions to commit the crime of simony. To be astounded at this among frail human beings would be naive indeed. The Church has legitimate reasons for

[11] "Absolutio pro mercatore, qui transportaverit hastas et alia prohibita ad partes infidelium et nullum lucrum reportavit taxatur 6 tur. Nota quod si lucrum reportaverit componit cum Datario et taxatur etc." "Et si percepit fructus ex illo, componit de fructibus perceptis cum Datari." E. Goller l. c. p. 166.

[12] Eci 31, 28; Pr. 22, 9; Da. 4, 24; Pr. 14, 21; Lu. 11, 4; Pr. 16, 6; Pr. 28, 27 etc.

[13] "Eleemosyna completa habet vim satisfactionis quam oratio, oratio quam jejunia. Et propter hoc eleemosyna magis indicitur ut universalis medicina pro peccatis quam alia" J. Friburgens, Summa Confessorum lib. III t. XXXIV, Q. 123. Cf. S. Antonii Summa p. 111 t. XIV c. 20 pars 3. Summa Sylvestrina s. v. Satisfactio.

[14] "Poenitentias peccunias sibi ipsis confessarii non applicent, neque a poenitentibus quidquam tamquam ministerii sui praemium petant vel accipiant."

demanding taxes and componenda, and true to her divine calling, she has ever taken the necessary means to stop abuses.[15]

Some writers strongly object to the laws of the Roman Index, which forbade the reading of tax-lists.[16] The Church has never refused permission to read forbidden books, when the petitioner was actuated by motives of scientific and sincere investigation. She rightly withholds some books from the curious and ignorant, who would derive no benefit from the reading and would peruse them only to their own detriment.

Other objections have been raised by zealous members of our own faith. St. Peter Damian deplored the fact that no layman can endure a fast of three days, and insisted that the penitential canons should be abolished if redemptions were not abrogated.[17] Pius II laments: "There is nothing that the Roman Curia gives without money. Even the imposition of hands and the gifts of the Holy Ghost are sold. The forgiveness of sin is only granted for coin."[18] In the year 1538 the cardinals drew up a plan for a general spiritual reformation in which they boldly declared that "the Penitentiaria and the Dataria were a refuge for the wicked, who there find impunity in return for money. The Church has assumed a right to maintain abuses so monstrous that they would destroy any human society."[19] The answer to these and similar objections, is contained in the last quotation. The Church of Christ is not merely a human society. She is guided by the Holy Ghost, the spirit of truth. If she were only human, no doubt she would have been destroyed long ago, through the greed and corruption of human agents. But in giving the history of any institution, why exaggerate its failing and minimize its works of mercy? The sources of God's teachings on Sinai and in the Cenaculum must always remain pure; the foundation of the Church, the pillars of truth must ever remain staunch. When adversities seemed to overwhelm them, St. Peter and his successors have cried out "*Lord save us, we perish*" (Matt.

---

[15] Ferraris, sub ver. Taxa. Hollweck, D. k. Strafg. p. 286. Cf. Ben. XIV De Synod. dioc. IV cap. 6n. 1.

[16] Appendix of Antwerp Index 1570 p. 69. Praxis et taxa officianae poenitentiariae Papae. Copied in Index of Sixtus V 1590. Clement VIII 1596 added "ab hereticis depravata." Benedict XIV adopted the formula "cum ab hereticis sit depravata": Index Benedict XIV, Romae 1758 p. 216.

[17] St. Petri Damiani Epist. lib, I, epist. 15. De modis poenitentiae. Wasserchleben, Bussordnungen n. 276, 341, 462.

[18] Aeneae Sylvii Lib. I Ep. 66 (Op. Basil, 1571). Doellinger, Beitrage zur politischen, kirchlichen Kulturgeschichte III 210.

[19] Le Plat, Monum. Concil. Trid. II, 601.

c. 8, v. 25), and the spirit of truth, that will guide the Church till the end of time, has ever come to their rescue. The successor of St. Peter, whose faith never wavers, shall ever confirm his brethren.

Since the time of Simon Magus the Church has found a remedy for every abuse. In the age of the martyrs, St. Cyprian severely reprehended the abuses made with the so-called "*libelli,*" yet he did not forbid the martyrs to give them. In later times abuses were always met by repressive measures on the part of the Church. The Council of Clovesho (747) condemned those penitents who imagined that crimes could be atoned by mercenary means.[20] The Lateran Council of 1215 restricted the excessive grants of Indulgences. The Council of Ravenna in the year 1317 enacted similar laws. Boniface IX in a letter to the bishop of Ferrara (1302), condemns the practice of certain religious who claimed authorization by the Pope to forgive all sorts of sins and exacted money from the simple-minded by promising perpetual happiness in this world and the next. Sixtus IV (1478) reserved a large number of indulgences formerly granted to confessors, lest the idea of gaining indulgences prove a greater incentive to sin. Pius III, when seeking advice from counsellors regarding the demands for reform of the Curia, received the following report: "Not for absolution but for the satisfaction money may be demanded, which is to be applied to pious purposes, as your Holiness has advised in numerous cases."[21] Finally the Council of Trent decreed that dispensation should be granted free of all charges.[22]

Diocesan Chanceries were bound to conform to this law and neither to exact nor accept anything but the modest contribution to the Chancery expenses sanctioned by an Instruction approved by Innocent XI (Oct. 8, 1678), reformed by Leo XIII (S. C. C. June, 1896) and known as the Innocentian Tax.[23] The executors of rescripts were always forbidden to receive or ask anything for the execution of matrimonial dispensations and customs to the contrary were tolerated rather than approved.[24] It cannot be

[20] Hadden & Stubbs Counc. III 373. Cf. Lingard Hist. and Antiquities of the Anglo Saxon Church, 2nd ed. London 1858, 1, 311.

[21] Doellinger, Beitrage zur polit, kirch. u. Kulturgeschichte III, 210.

[22] Sess. XXIV, c. V, De Ref. Matr.

[23] Wernz, vol. IV, n. 634, note 166; Giovini, t. II, p. 109; Feije, n. 690; Kirchenlex. t. III, p. 771; Ojetti, Syn. Taxa; Ferraris, Prompta Bibl. Taxa; Bouix, de Episc. II, p. 5, s. 30, par. 1.

[24] Gasparri, n. 398; Wernz, n. 639, note 207; Pützer, p. 88; S. C. C. June 20, 1871; Jan. 28, 1822; S. Penitent. Apr. 20, 1861; S. C. C. Apr. 18, 1883. Concil. plen. Balt. III (a. 1884 n. 134).

said that the discipline of our episcopal Curias is in contradiction to the various instructions of the Holy See declaring that dispensations are to be granted gratuitously. Bishops generally in virtue of indults demand taxes for the expenses incurred and the support of good works, never for the dispensation itself or for the profit of the one who grants or executes the rescript.

In the New Code, canon 1056, we read: Ordinaries and their officials may not demand any emolument, when granting a dispensation, with the exception of a small offering for defraying the expenses of the Chancery in dispensations for those, who are not poor, unless a faculty herefor be granted them expressly by the Holy See, and if they shall have exacted anything, they are held to restitution. All customs to the contrary are hereby declared illegal. No other charges are therefore permitted except the small fee for defraying the expenses of the Chancery, though this offering may be used for any purpose. Special faculties mentioned in the Code are enjoyed by many bishops in this country. In virtue of the extraordinary faculties under Form T. no. 15, bishops can ask a modest offering for good works.

Canon 1507 demands that all regulations concerning taxes, which are to be paid in ecclesiastical provinces for the various acts of voluntary jurisdiction or for the execution of apostolic rescripts or upon the occasion of the administration of Sacraments and Sacramentals, are to be drawn up in the provincial council, or at the meeting of the bishops of the province, but the statutes have no force of law without the approbation of the Apostolic See.

Bishops generally dispense gratuitously in the forum of conscience, but they are not forbidden to ask and accept a just remuneration for the expenses incurred in verifying facts or in seeking the necessary information.[25] As to the present procedure of the S. Penitentiaria, it follows the rules set down in the Constitution "In apostolicae" (Benedict XIV) and "Sapienti consilio." Accordingly, its business is transacted with the greatest secrecy and entirely gratuitously (Omnino secreto et gratis).

---

[25] Gasparri, n. 398; Wernz, n. 639, note 207; Putzer, p. 88; S. C. C. June 20, 1871; Jan 28, 1822; S. Penitent. Apr. 20, 1861.

SOURCES AND BIBLIOGRAPHY

Sources

Act Apostolicae Sedis. Commentarium officiale, Rome.
Acta Sanctae Sedis. Rome, 1865, etc.
Adami Perseniae Abbatis Epist. XXVI, Rome, 1662.
Archiv fur katholisches Kirchenrecht, Mainz.
Canoniste Contemporain, Paris.
Corpus iuris canonici ed. Leibzig, 1839. Freiburg, 1879.
Const. Synod. Odonis Episc. Paris, 1198.
Concil. Rothomagense, Bessin, 1717.
Catholic Encyclopedia, N. Y., 1912.
Constitutio Richardi Episcopi Sarum, 1217.
Collectanea S. C. de P. F. Rome, 1893.
Concilii plen. Baltimorensis tertii. Acta et Decreta, Baltimore, 1884.
Codex Iuris Canonici, Rome, 1917.
Ecclesiastical Review, Philadelphia.
English Historical Review, 1893.
Formularium S. C. S. O.
Katholik, Mainz.
Liber Diurnus RR. PP. ed. Duchesne, Paris, 1891.
Le Plat, Monument Concil. Trid.
Lintzer Quartalschrift.
Nouvelle Revue theologique, Tournalis.
Martin Collectio documentorum Conc. Vat. Paderborn, 1873.
Summa Magistri Rolandi, ed. Thaner, Insbruck, 1875.
Summa Sylvestriana.
Vaticanum Archivum Armarium.

Authors

Ballerini-Palmieri, Opus theologicum morale, Prato, 1890.
Baumgarten, Leo's Historical Writings, N. Y., 1909.
Bargilliat, Praelectiones Iuris Can. ed. 30, Paris, 1915.
Battifol, Les pretres penitentier romains. Compte rendu du Congres de catholiques a Bruxelles II, 1894.
Bellarmine, R. S. J. Opera omnia, Paris, 1872.
Benedict XIV. De Synodo dioc. Rome, 1748; Bullarium, Rome, 1754-58.
Berengar, Die Ablaesse, Paderborn, 1900.
Bouix, D. Tractatus de Curia Rom. Paris, 1880.
Capello, F. M. De Curia Rom. Rome, 1913.
Corradus Pyrrhus, Praxis Dispensationum Apostolicarum, Venice, 1669.

D'Annibale, In Const. Apostolicae Sedis commentarii, Prato, 1894; Summula Theol. Moralis, Rome, 1892.

De Justis, De Dispensationibus Matrimonialibus, Lucae, 1691.

De Luca, Relatio cur. Romanae, Venice, 1759.

Denifle, Die aelteste Taxrolle der ap. Poenitentiarie, Archiv f. Litt. u. Kirch. 1888.

De Smet, Betrothment and Marriage, B. Herder. Translated from the French, 1912.

Doellinger, Beitrage zur polit. kirch, und Kulturgeschichte, 1862.

Dupin, De St. Andre, Taxe de la Penitencerie apost. d'après l'edition publiee d Paris, 1620, Paris, 1879.

Eubel, Archiv fur kathol. Kirchenrecht 1890 vol. 54; Der Registerband d. Kard. Grosspoenitent. Bentevenga im Arch. f. k. K. XIV, Mainz, 1890.

Fagnanus, P. Ius can, seu commentarii in V lib. decret. Rome, 1661.

Feije, De Imped, et Disp. Matr. Louvain ed. 4, 1893.

Ferreres, Los Esp. y el Matr. Madrid, 1916; La Curia Rom. Madrid, 1911.

Ferraris, Bibliotheca, Rome, 1885-1896.

Gennari-Boudinhon, Consult. moral. Paris, 1912.

Gonzalez, M. Commentaria perpetua in singulos textus Iuris can., Lyons, 1673.

Gasparri, P. Tractatus Canonicus De Matrimonio, Paris, 1904, ed. 3.

Genicot-Salmanticenses, ed. 6, Brussels, 1909.

Gibbings, The Tax of the Apostolic Penitentiaria, Dublin, 1872.

Giovini, De Dispensat. matrim. Naples, 1863.

Giraldi, Expositio Iuris Pontificii, Rome, 1769.

Goeller, E. Die paepstliche Poenitentiarie von ihrem Ursprung bis zu ihrer Umgestaltung durch Pius V, Rome, 1907.

Green, Indulg., Sacram. Absolution and Tax Tables, London, 1872.

Gomez, Tractatus de potestate Poenitentiariae, Venice, 1557.

Gury, J. P. Compendium theol. moralis, Paris, 1862.

Guilaume le Breton Philippeide, ed. Delaborde, Paris, 1885.

Hadden and Stubbs, Councils and ecclesiastical documents, Oxford, 1871.

Haskins, C. The sources for the history of the papal Penitentiaria, American Journal of Theology IX, a. 1905.

Hinschius, System des kathol. Kirchenrechts, Berlin, 1869.

Hollweck, Kirchliche Strafgesetze, Mainz, 1899.

Index Benedicti XIV, Rome, 1758.

Lea, C. History of Auricular Confession, Philadelphia, 1898; A Formulary of the Papal Penitentiaria in the thirteenth century, Phila. 1892.

Lega, De Iudiciis, Praelectiones in text. Iur. can. Rome, 1898.

Lehmkuhl, Theologia moralis, ed. II, Freiburg, 1910.

Leitner, Praelectiones Iuris can. Ratisbon 1904. Lehrbuch, Paderborn,, 1902.

Lingard, History and Antiquities of the Anglo Saxon Ch. London, 1858, ed. 2.

Noldin, H. Summa Theol. Mor. N. Y. Pustet, 1906.

Ojetti, De Curia Rom. Rome, 1910; Synopsis Rerum, ed. 3, Rome, 1912.

Pastor, Geschichte der Paepste, Freiburg, Herder, 1886.

Pesch, C. Praelectiones dogmaticae, Freiburg, Herder, 1909.

Phillips, Lehrbuch des Kirchenrechts, 1859-1862.

Pirhing, E. Ius can. in V lib. Decretalium, Dillingen, 1645.

Plettenberg, Notitia Congregat. et tribunal. Hildesheim, 1693.

Pohle, Lehrbuch der Dogmatik, Paderborn, 1906.

Putzer, Commentarium in Facultates Apostolicas, Benziger, N. Y., 1893.

Reiffenstuel, O. F. M. Ius canonicum universum, Munich, 1702-1714.

Riganti, J. B. Commentarium in regulas Tournais, 1751.

Rosset, De Sacramento Matr. Paris, 1895.

Sabetti-Barrett, Pustet, 1906, 1917.

Saegmuller, Lehrbuch des kathol, Kirchenrechts, Freiburg ed. 2, 1909; Die. Thaetigkeit und Stellung der Kardinaele bis Papst Bonifaz, Freiburg, 1896.

Salmanticenses, Cursus Theologiae Moralis, Lugduni, 1879.

Sanchez, Disputationum de S. Matrimonii Sacramento, Antwerp, 1626.

Santi, F. Praelectiones Iuris Can. N. Y., Pustet, 1886.

Scavini, Theologia Moralis, Paris, 1867.

Scherer, R. Handbuch des Kirchenrechts, 1886.

Schmalzgrueber, S. J. Ius ecclesiasticum universum, Ingolstadt, 1716.

Schneider, J. Rescripta authentica, Ratisbon, 1885.

Schnitzer, Katholisches Eherecht, Freiburg, 1898.

Sozomen, Historia Ecclesiastica, Oxford, 1860; Post Nicene Fathers, N. Y., 1890.

Socrates, Historia Ecclesiastica, Oxford, 1860; Post Nicene Fathers, N. Y., 1890.

St. Alphonsus Liguori, Theologia Moralis, Rome, 1905.

Stiegler, M. Dispensation, Dispensationswesen und Dispensationsrecht im Kirchenrecht; Geschichte der Dispensationstaxen, Mainz, 1901.

Suarez, De legibus, Coimbra, 1612.

Thomassin, Vetus et nova disciplina, Paris, 1688.

St. Thomas, Opera omnia, Rome, 1882.

Taunton, E. The Law of the Church, London, 1906.

Telch, C. Epitome Theologiae moralis, ed. 2. N. Y., Pustet, 1913.

Vermeersch, Ne temere, De Forma Sponsalium ac Matrimonii, Bruges, 1908.

Vermeersch, De Religiosis Institutis et personis, Bruges, 1907.

Van der Acker, Decreti Ne temere. . . . Interpretatio, Buscoduci, (Bois-le Duc), 1909.

Vogt, Das kirchliche Eherecht, ed. 3, Koeln, 1910.

Weber, Rev. N. A., S. M. Simony in the Christian Church, Baltimore, 1909.

Wouters, Commentarium in Decretum Ne temere, Rome, ed. 3, 1910.

Wernz, S. J. Ius Decretalium, Prato, 1912-1915.

Zitelli, De Dispensationibus matrimonialibus, Rome, 1887.

Universitas Catholica Americae

Washingtonii, D. C.

S. Facultas Theologica

1917-1918

No. 5

TITULI

Deus Lux Mea

TITULI

QUOS AD DOCTORATUS GRADUM IN

IURE CANONICO

APUD
UNIVERSITATEM CATHOLICAM AMERICAE

CONSEQUENDAM PUBLICE PROPUGNABIT

GULIELMUS JOANNES KUBELBECK
Saceredos Diocesis Superiorensis
Iuris Canonici Licentiatus

HORA IX A. M. DIE VI JUNII A. D. MCMXVIII

I. De legibus ecclesiasticis.
II. De consuetudine.
III. De rescriptis.
IV. De privilegiis.
V. De dispensationibus.
VI. De clericis in genere.
VII. De excardinatione et incardinatione.
VIII. De obligatione clericorum.
IX. De potestate ordinaria et delegata.
X. De S. C. S. Officii.
XI. De S. C. Concilii.
XII. De S. C. de Disciplina Sacramentorum.
XIII. De origine S. Poenitentiariae.
XIV. De constitutione S. Poenitentiariae.
XV. De competentia S. Poenitentiariae.
XVI. De impedimento occulto.
XVII. De relatione S. Poenitentiariae ad facultates Ordinarii.
XVIII. De relatione S. Poenitentiariae ad facultates parochi et confessarii.
XIX. Quomodo sit recurrendum ad S. Poenitentiariam.
XX. De indulgentiis.
XXI. De taxis.
XXII. De componendis.
XXIII. De electione Episcoporum in Statibus Foederatis.
XXIV. De Synodo dioecesana.
XXV. De Vicario Generali.
XXVI. De cancellario aliisque notariis et archivo episcopali.
XXVII. De examinatoribus synodalibus et parochis consultoribus.
XXVIII. De consultoribus dioecesanis.
XXIX. De vicariis foraneis.
XXX. De iuribus parochorum.
XXXI. De vicariis cooporatoribus.
XXXII. De ecclesiarum rectoribus.
XXXIII. De obligatione et privilegiis religiosi paroeciam regentis.
XXXIV. De transitu ad aliam religionem.
XXXV. De egressu e religione.
XXXVI. De societatibus sive virorum sive mulierum in communi viventium sine votis.
XXXVII. De patrinis.

XXXVIII. De Missarum eleemosynis seu stipendiis.
XXXIX. De ministro sacrae poenitentiae.
XL. De reservatione peccatorum.
XLI. De ministro extremae unctionis.
XLII. De requisitis in subiecto sacrae ordinationis.
XLIII. De iis, quae matrimonii celebratione praemitti debent.
XLIV. De impedimento ligaminis.
XLV. De impedimento impotentiae.
XLVI. De convalidatione matrimonii.
XLVII. De diebus festis.
XLVIII. De abstinentia et ieiunio.
XLIX. De prohibtione librorum.
L. De iudice.
LI. De actore et reo convento.
LII. De peritis.
LIII. De modo procedendi in remotione parochorum inamovibilium.
LIV. De modo procedendi in suspensione ex informata conscientia infligenda.
LV. De natura delicti eiusque divisione.
LVI. De imputabilitate delicti, de causis illam agravantibus vel minuentibus.
LVII. De excommunicatione.
LVIII. De suspensione.
LIX. De delictis contra vitam, libertatem, proprietatem, bonam famam ac bonos mores.
LX. De abusu potestatis vel officii ecclesiastici.

Vidit Sacra Facultas:

EDMUND T. SHANAHAN, Ph. D., S. T. D., J. C. L., p. t. Decanus.

JOHN A. RYAN, S. T. D., p. t. a Secretis.

Vidit Rector Universitatis,

✠ THOMAS I. SHAHAN, S. T. D.

VITA

William John Kubelbeck was born of Catholic parents in Kaltenbach, a village of Bohemia, May 4th, 1883. When eight years of age he came with his parents to the United States. He received his elementary education in St. Mary's School, Port Washington, Wisconsin. His petition to study for the priesthood at the Pontifical College Josephinum, was granted by the Rt. Rev. Rector Joseph Jessing. After the usual college and seminary courses, he was ordained priest for the diocese of Superior, Wisconsin, by the Rt. Rev. James J. Hartley, D. D., Bishop of Columbus, May 19, 1910. After five years of parish work he was sent to Washington, D. C., for a post-graduate course in the Sacred Sciences at the Catholic University of America. His major study was Canon Law under the direction of the Rt. Rev. F. Bernardini, S. T. D., J. U. D. His minor studies were Sociology and Apologetics under the direction of Rev. W. J. Kerby, S. T. L., LL. D., and Very Rev. C. F. Aiken, S. T. D., respectively.

He desires to express at this opportunity his sincere thanks to his professors and the members of the Faculty of Sacred Science for their kind assistance.

www.ingramcontent.com/pod-product-compliance
Lightning Source LLC
LaVergne TN
LVHW050205080826
844660LV00012B/362

* 9 7 8 0 8 1 3 2 2 1 9 6 0 *